W9-BIZ-055

The Big Book of Pop Culture

THE BIG BOOK OF POP CULTURE

A How-to Guide for Young Artists

HAL NIEDZVIECKI

Illustrated by Marc Ngui

annick press
toronto + new york + vancouver

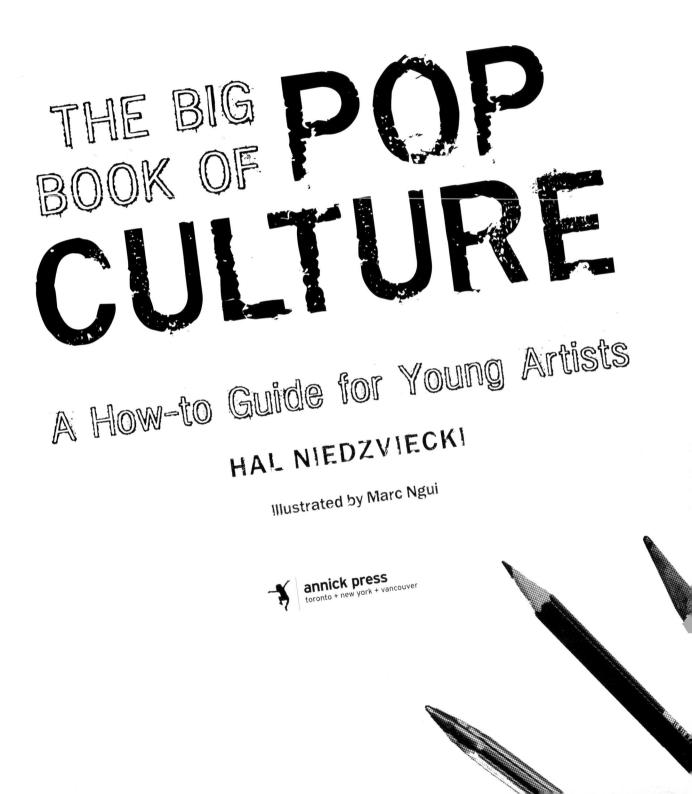

Text © 2007 Hal Niedzviecki
Illustrations © 2007 Marc Ngui

Annick Press Ltd.

All rights reserved. No part of this work covered by the copyrights hereon may be reproduced or used in any form or by any means—graphic, electronic, or mechanical—without prior written permission of the publisher.

We acknowledge the support of the Canada Council for the Arts, the Ontario Arts Council, the Government of Canada through the Book Publishing Industry Development Program (BPIDP), and the Ontario Book Publishing Tax Credit (OBPTC) for our publishing activities.

Edited by Pam Robertson
Copy-edited and proofread by John Sweet
Cover and interior illustrations by Marc Ngui
Photo research by Hal Niedzviecki and Antonia Banyard
Cover and interior design by Naomi MacDougall

Every effort has been made to trace copyright holders and gain permission for use of images within this book. If there are any inadvertent omissions, please contact the publisher.

Cataloging in Publication
Niedzviecki, Hal, 1971–
The big book of pop culture : a how-to guide for young artists /
by Hal Niedzviecki ; illustrated by Marc Ngui.

Includes index.
ISBN-13: 978-1-55451-056-6 (bound) · ISBN-10: 1-55451-056-2 (bound)
ISBN-13: 978-1-55451-055-9 (pbk.) · ISBN-10: 1-55451-055-4 (pbk.)

1. Popular culture—Juvenile literature. 2. Creation (Literary, artistic, etc.)—Juvenile literature. 3. Arts and teenagers—Juvenile literature. 4. Arts and youth—Juvenile literature. I. Ngui, Marc, 1972– II. Title.

NX163.N53 2007   J700.835   C2006-906229-3

Distributed in Canada by Firefly Books Ltd.
66 Leek Crescent
Richmond Hill, ON
L4B 1H1

Published in the U.S.A. by Annick Press (U.S.) Ltd.
Distributed in the U.S.A. by
Firefly Books (U.S.) Inc.
P.O. Box 1338
Ellicott Station
Buffalo, NY 14205

Printed and bound in China

Visit our website at www.annickpress.com

CONTENTS

INTRODUCTION   No One Understands Me Even Though I'm the Only One in the Whole World Who Has a Clue, and Other Thoughts on Your Exceptional Creativity (7)

Using This Book (8)

PART ONE   Everything You Need to Know Before You Make Your Own Pop Culture

CHAPTER 1   I Know It When I See It: Pop's Past, Present, and Future (13)

CHAPTER 2   Attack of the Blob! Pop Culture Everywhere (35)

CHAPTER 3   Your Global Neighborhood Needs You: Creating DIY Pop Culture (53)

PART TWO   From Acting to Zines: The A~Zs of Making Your Own Pop Culture

CHAPTER 4   Starting the Presses: Zines, Comics, Books (77)

CHAPTER 5   Moving the Picture: Making Your Own Cheap, Wonderful, and Probably Pretty Weird Movies, Shows, and Videos (101)

CHAPTER 6   Pop Music's Not Dead: It Just Needs a (DIY) Revolution (125)

CHAPTER 7   Shocking the System: Radio, TV, the Web (147)

Image Credits (180)

Index (182)

About the Author (183)

No One Understands Me Even Though I'm the Only One in the Whole World Who Has a Clue, and Other Thoughts on Your Exceptional Creativity

Ever feel like you just don't care? I mean, you're watching TV or flipping through a magazine and you realize that you *really* don't care: about what celebrities are wearing, or how many cylinders this year's sports car has, or what grisly crime is going to be solved by a bunch of hunky detectives in designer outfits.

Sometimes it seems as if there's this whole world of pop culture that tells you what to care about but has nothing whatsoever to do with your life.

At the same time, we're constantly told that we should be original and creative and fantastic. But how did being original and fantastic come to mean talking about stuff that we don't care about and pretending to solve outlandish crimes while keeping our hair perfectly gelled? What's so great about that?

Pop culture bombards us with stories, songs, shows, movies, and products that tell us to be ourselves and tap into our creativity and talent. But when we *are* creative and original, we find out that no one is interested unless we're doing the same stuff as everyone else. Unless you're trying out for the latest reality TV singing show, no one wants you on TV. Unless you're some wild and wacky character with an amazing gimmick, you don't get any attention. But what if you don't

want to be totally brand new and ultracool and original? What if you just want to be you?

Creativity is often confused with originality. But when you create, the challenge *isn't* to think of something no one has ever done before; it's to figure out what you want to say and why you want to say it. Creativity is about discovering who you are, including how much *like* other people you are.

This is a book about creating a space where you get to say what you care about. This is a book about using pop culture to communicate how *you* see the world and how *you* want the world to see you. You'll learn how to use pop culture to create your own TV shows, magazines, websites, songs— whatever you want.

A lot of people seem to think that just being who they are isn't interesting enough. But you have the right to be normal, you have the right to make mistakes, and you have the right to not want to be a superstar. And most important of all, you have the right to create your own pop culture your way, for yourself. Even if no one ever hears our songs, reads our zines, or watches our movies, expressing ourselves just because we feel like it is something we all have the right to do.

So what *are* you going to do?

I started my own magazine in 1995. I called it *Broken Pencil* and it's still publishing today. The

magazine is all about how much I love independent pop culture—zines, blogs, movies, music, websites, and more. When I started the magazine, I had only the slightest idea about how many people were doing creative things and wanted to share them. Now, people I've worked on the magazine with are some of my best friends. And I've met creators from all over the world who produce amazing comics, video games, music, and zines—stuff I'd never have known about if I hadn't decided to just go ahead and do something.

What I did wasn't all that amazing, or even original. But it was what I wanted to do. Because it meant a lot to me, I worked hard at it and kept it going, and eventually it started to mean something to other people too. Not because I'm such an original genius, but because we need, in our world, more places where people can be creative—where we can express ourselves—without feeling all kinds of pressure.

So this book is part of what I started years ago, when I wasn't that much older than you are now. And even after all those years, I still need to be reminded that pop culture isn't just a way to talk about the rich and famous. There's another kind of pop culture out there—the kind I started my magazine to celebrate. It's a pop culture that lets you share your stories and ideas with people all over the world.

Not that anyone cares.

But then again, you never know.

Using This Book

The Big Book of Pop Culture is divided into two parts. The first part contains thoughts and ideas about how pop culture works and why you should make your own. This section is best read in order, but feel free to skip ahead if you already know the difference between *culture jamming*, *do-it-yourself*, *underground*, and *plunder*. In fact, if you know all that stuff, I should be reading your book!

The second part of this book is about starting pop culture projects, including topics like publishing your own magazine, putting out your own CD of songs, or running your own radio station. This section doesn't have to be read in order; just flip through and stop whenever you see something that interests you.

Pop culture—making it, understanding it, thinking about its effect on our lives—is a huge topic. This book can't tell you everything you need to know, which is why each chapter ends with bits and pieces meant to help you keep going on your own. So, to encourage what the schools like to call "self-directed learning," all chapters of the book have the following:

FURTHER READING Pretty obvious. Books or websites to check out that will take you deeper into the ideas discussed in the chapter. Some of these books aren't written for teens (of course, you can and should read them anyway), so you might want to bring your dictionary to help with words like *phonograph* and *post-rock*. For the less adventurous, books written specifically for young adults will have a star (★) next to them.

DO IT YOURSELF Projects you can do in a half day or so. These simple, fun tasks are meant to help you discover how you can harness the power of pop culture to explore what you and your community are really about (other than a mall, fast-food restaurants, and big box stores that sell 300 rolls of toilet paper in one giant pack). These suggested activities come with a promise: you'll have fun and learn all kinds of cool things. Anyway, don't take my word for it: do it yourself.

KEYWORD SEARCH Things happen so fast in pop culture. By the time you get around to reading this book, a new trend will have started that I didn't even know about yet. So, to stay on top of the latest developments in making your own blog or recording your band's music, it's a good idea to look for up-to-the-minute information by doing web searches on sites like Creative Commons or Google. Start with the suggested keywords provided and then move on to other words and phrases that, horrors, you'll have to think up all by yourself.

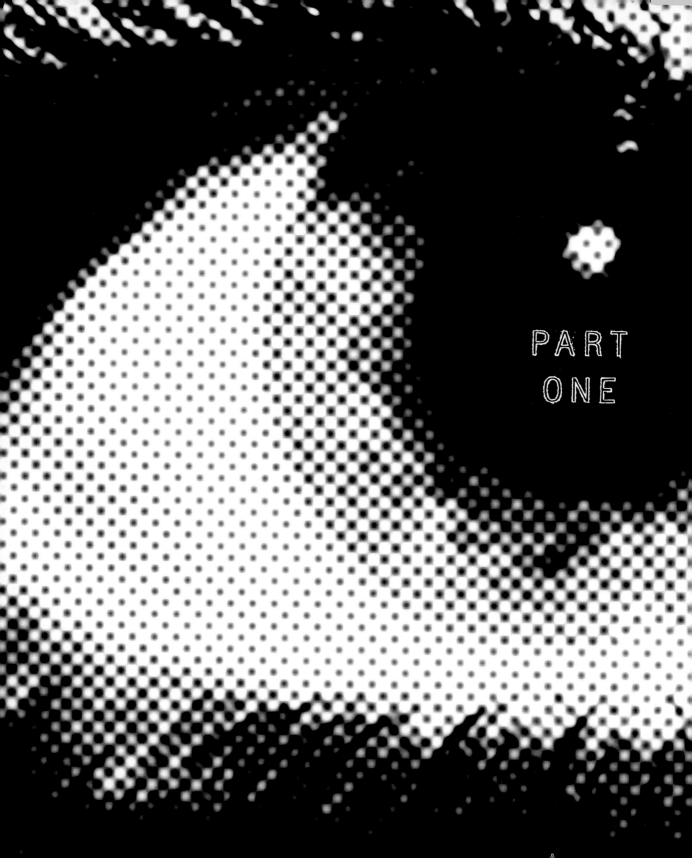

PART
ONE

EVERYTHING YOU NEED TO KNOW Before You Make Your Own Pop Culture

I Know It
When I See It

Pop's Past, Present, and Future

What is Pop Culture? (And Why Should You Care Anyway?)

You wouldn't think that you were going to become a mathematician if you didn't understand how to add. And you'd never imagine that you could just take the stage at the concert hall and play classical piano without years of lessons. So why would you think about making pop culture without spending some time learning how it works? It'd be like watching a television show about emergency room doctors and then figuring that you're ready to operate.

So, go ahead, tell me: what exactly is pop culture?

Huh. How about that. All of a sudden the room gets real quiet.

Yeah, okay, you know it when you see it. And you do see it. Every day. Every moment of the day, if you had your way and there was nobody around to tell you to turn off the TV, walk away from that computer screen, save the game, and would you please turn down that terrible music?

But just because we can recognize something and understand it doesn't mean we know what, exactly, it is and how to do it ourselves.

So let's begin at the very beginning:

Pop culture is short for *popular culture*. Which raises two obvious questions: 1) What is popular? and 2) What is culture?

Let's start with the question of culture. Culture is the way we live in our societies. Culture is what we believe, what kind of government we have, what we eat for dinner, and what we do for fun—all that stuff makes up our culture. Culture is a lot like a book. A book has a value that is much more than a bunch of paper glued together. A book wouldn't be a book if it was just blank pages; what makes it valuable are the ideas and stories printed on the pages. Such ideas and stories are how we represent our culture. If you want to tell your own stories, then what you really want to do is express your own culture. Your culture is how you live, and how people live is what stories, songs, and artworks are all about. What this really means is that anyone and everyone can and should make culture. We all like to tell stories about who we are and how we live.

Now that we have an idea of what culture is, we can deal with that other, far more familiar word—*popular*. Popular are those kids at school with the white teeth and the tan even in winter and the name-brand clothing and the pretty hair and the expensive cell phones and the friends all around them who look the same and laugh the same way and—Wow, sorry, got carried away there! Anyway, you get the idea. *Popular* is a word to describe those people and things that everybody wants to know about and get their hands on. So, popular culture is, in a way, the newest, flashiest, coolest kid on the block. It's the culture that everybody talks about, as in, "Did you see that movie yet?" "Did you check out that weird website?" "You've *got* to listen to this song."

Culture is the words and pictures in the book (or on the screen or on the disc) telling the stories of how we live our lives. And popular culture is all about the stories that really get everyone's attention.

Two Important Ideas:
Accessible and Mass Produced

So now we know what pop culture is. Great. Let's get down to business, making the next *Pirates of the Caribbean* or becoming the next Pink.

Hold on, though. If it were that easy, we'd all be superstars riding in limos, wouldn't we?

There are still things we have to understand about pop culture before we get started making our own. Remember when I defined pop culture by saying it was the stories and other representations of our culture that were most available and popular? Well, I've just thought of a problem with that. Here I am writing a book about how you can make your own pop culture movies and music and magazines, and then I go and tell you that pop culture has to be really appealing to tons of people. There's a contradiction: if you aren't getting lots of attention and popularity (which you probably won't be if you're just starting out), then you aren't making *pop* culture, right?

Obviously, we have a problem with this word *popular*. And the answer is to understand that *popular*, at least when it is attached to the word *culture*, doesn't always have to mean "something that everybody knows, wants, or has." In this case it has a different meaning, more like "*able to reach* a lot of people" than "*has reached* millions of people who just can't get enough." To understand the difference, we need to make sense of two concepts: *accessible* and *mass produced*.

ACCESSIBLE

Being accessible is what puts the "pop" in popular. If you record a song of you muttering things no one can understand set to the sound of you smashing light bulbs, that song isn't going to be

very accessible. No one will get it. Accessible culture is culture that a lot of people are able to "get." A television sitcom is far more accessible than an opera or a ballet. Sitcoms are on every television station every night of the week, and you don't usually have to pay much attention to "get" them. But if you see ballet or opera (either live or on television), you are probably not going to understand it right away. You would need background information—some knowledge of the history and meaning of what was being performed. Which is why a sitcom anyone can watch and get is considered accessible while the opera is often not.

You can see why *accessible* is such an important word. Popular culture is culture that, because of its accessibility, has the potential to be appreciated by anybody. The tormented young man with a penchant for recording the poetry of light bulb smashing might very well be communicating something worthwhile, but what he's communicating isn't likely to become pop culture. But if you tell the story of an unhappy young man muttering into a tape recorder and breaking light bulbs who is saved by a caring classmate who realizes the guy is really a good person and just needs a

friend, that story will be accessible. It's accessible because it has characters and a plot that are pretty familiar to us.

MASS PRODUCED

Of course, for anybody to encounter pop culture, they have to be able to not just get it but also get their hands on it. This brings us to the idea of mass production. *Mass produced* means that something is created specifically to be a product that can reach huge numbers of people. Light bulbs are mass produced, as are cars, computers, and every single item in the local convenience store.

All pop culture is mass produced in some way. The fact that it is mass produced doesn't necessarily mean that millions of every product are sold all over the world. But it does mean that the content of any given pop culture item, whether it's a movie or a website or a song, has *built into it* the ability to be reproduced over and over again. Think of it like this: A performance of a ballet is not something that can be easily and instantly duplicated for as many people as want it. There are a limited number of seats in the theater and a limited number of performances. In contrast, the whole

idea of making a movie is to create something that, by its very nature, can be shown to as many people as want to see it. Those ballet dancers would get plenty tired if they had to perform their show five times every day in thousands of movie theaters all over the world, not to mention jump up and do their show in someone's living room every time the ballet was rented at the video store.

Unlike the ballet or, for instance, an oil painting such as Leonardo da Vinci's *Mona Lisa*, Hollywood movies, romance novels, rap songs, and video games like the Halo series are all created to be mass produced and sent around the world for as many people as want them. Websites and digital song files like MP3s are mass produced instantaneously, without even having to be made at a factory. Even if only a single person visits a website, there is still the *potential* for a million people to drop by and check it out. This potential defines mass production and sets pop culture apart from culture.

Pop Culture Cheat Sheet

So, what is pop culture? This isn't a test, but let's review anyway, just for the fun of it. So far we've established three important facts about pop:

❶ IT CAN'T JUST BE AN OBJECT. A house isn't pop culture, a pair of blue socks isn't pop culture, a blank CD-ROM or a book with no writing in it isn't

pop culture. These are simply functional objects. They don't come with content—an idea or set of ideas that creates emotions, experiences, and stories that express our culture.

❷ POP CULTURE IS ACCESSIBLE. In other words, even if we come across an object that also has cultural content, such as a video of a ballet, if the content is too weird or too difficult or too far removed from the everyday, it is not accessible. If it isn't accessible, it isn't pop culture.

❸ POP CULTURE IS ABLE TO BE MASS PRODUCED quickly and easily in a way that could potentially reach a lot of people.

Rethinking the Definitions: You Decide

Those three key elements of pop culture make a lot of sense when you're trying to define it. But the thing that we like about pop culture is the way it's always changing and surprising us. One minute something is popular, the next minute it's not. One day everyone is throwing their sweaty body into the mosh pit, the next day we're all heading out for late night karaoke.

Just exactly why some part of our culture becomes popular and another part gets sent to the basement to gather dust is still up for debate. Who decides if something is accessible? Really, it's up to you.

The Pop Prof:
An Interview with Imre Szeman

IMRE SZEMAN IS a professor of English and cultural studies and co-wrote the book *Popular Culture: A User's Guide* with Susie O'Brien. We tracked him down to get the higher-education take on pop culture.

You wrote a whole university textbook about pop culture. Why are people studying it?

First, we want to understand what makes popular culture so "popular." What does it take to create pop culture? How does popular culture relate to other forms of culture (so-called "high" culture, things like novels, fine art, classical music, and so on)? These are the kinds of questions that those who study popular culture might ask. The second reason is that pop culture circulates important ideas about how we understand ourselves and our societies. It is tempting to assume that pop culture is "just" entertainment, "just" what we do after we finish with our work, a harmless way to relax. But we learn as much from pop culture as we do from being in school or from our families—probably more. While pop culture doesn't teach us calculus, it's one of the main places that we learn about

what relationships are supposed to be like, what kinds of people and activities are valued (and valuable) and what aren't, and what it means to be men and women. We tend to imagine pop culture as being something far away from "reality." But pop culture shapes reality in ways that we are not always aware of.

What's the first thing people immediately "get" about pop culture?

They get that it's about pleasures, iden- tities, and experience, but also that it's often about money and profit.

People are always blaming pop culture for, it seems, everything. Is pop culture really that bad?

There is a tendency to use pop culture as a punching bag for everything that's wrong in the world. It's true that popular culture is a powerful force in society, but it isn't always bad. That's far too simple. Still, it's a mistake to say that pop culture doesn't have any effect. Pop culture is about fun in a world that is often boring. It's dominated by themes of individual freedom. These themes are an important part of how we see the world, and how we think we might be able to improve things happening around us.

How do you think pop culture will be different in 50 years?

There's no doubt that, as with everything else, pop culture will change over time. New technologies will have a role to play—when film emerged, it would have been impossible to imagine DVD players in minivans. There is also likely to be more pop culture, and more non-Western pop culture too.

At the same time, I think that the position of pop culture in society won't change as much as we might expect. Complaints about pop culture haven't changed very much over the last century. In the 1920s, people were already complaining about there being too much consumption in our culture, too much emphasis in pop culture on people buying more and more stuff. Sounds familiar, doesn't it?

We all know the story of Dracula, that mythical Lord of the Vampires who spends his nights looking for victims to quench his undying thirst. In some ways, you might say that vampires are a pretty weird idea, and maybe not something everyone would relate to. And yet, since Irish writer Bram Stoker's book *Dracula* was published in 1897, there's been a steady stream of movies, TV shows, books, theme park rides, and comic books about vampires, and Dracula is now one of pop culture's most recognizable, mass-produced, and accessible scary monsters.

Different kinds of cultural experiences feed off pop culture. A few years ago there was a ballet based on *Dracula* that played in cities around North America. Is the ballet version of *Dracula* pop culture? Come to think of it, never mind the ballet (for the reasons stated earlier, about tired dancers); what about the film of that same ballet? Is a movie of a ballet based on that very popular and accessible story pop culture? A ballet company might use the story of Dracula to try to make their shows more accessible and appealing in order to attract a bigger audience. This, of course, makes it harder and harder to define where pop culture ends and so-called high culture, like the ballet or the opera, begins.

Another problem connected with trying to define pop culture is the idea of it being both an object—something you pick up at the store like a jug of milk—and also something that creates feelings in us through the story it tells and the characters it helps us to imagine. Now, is a box of cereal with a recognizable cartoon character on it part of pop culture, or is it just a box containing something you eat for breakfast? You've seen Lucky the Leprechaun and Tony the Tiger plenty of times in commercials. They are part of pop culture—cartoon characters that are engaging, mass produced, and accessible. But they mostly appear in cartoon commercials for cereal, not in movies or television shows. Sometimes it's hard to distinguish between pop culture and an object like a simple box of cereal.

Because pop culture is involved with so many aspects of our lives—what we wear, what we eat, how we get around, where we work, and of course what we do for fun—it's often hard to know just what is or isn't part of that slippery creature. This is a good thing. When something is hard to define, that means society has not yet figured out its exact role or purpose. For us, this means we can still be part of defining what pop culture is and how it works. It's up to us to get in there and change what people think about pop culture, and how they think it should work, by creating our own movies, magazines, and radio shows.

A Brief History of Pop Culture

So it turns out that pop culture doesn't have an exact definition. Well, guess what? Pop culture doesn't exactly have a history either. And guess what else? Understanding the "not exact" history of pop culture is going to help us get to know how and why we should create our own.

History that has to do with culture is not like the history of a country; it doesn't have a straightforward timeline. We know that World War II began in 1939 and ended in 1945. But pop culture doesn't have a start date and it certainly doesn't have a completion date. After all, it's still waiting for your contribution...

Technology and Accessibility

On page 23 there is a timeline that charts some important dates in the development of pop culture. Looking at it, you can see that most of pop culture's early history had to do with the invention of new technologies. Obviously, there couldn't be movies until someone invented a way to make moving pictures.

But just because something was invented doesn't meant that—presto!—mass entertainment came into being. First the invented technology had to become cheap enough and popular enough for lots of people to use it. Movies weren't pop culture until there were movie theaters, and there weren't movie theaters until the technology was available to show movies in such a way that many people could afford to go to them. The German goldsmith Johannes Gutenberg invented the printing press in 1436, but it would be at least 400 years before enough people could read and afford books and newspapers to make printed matter a cultural staple.

So, even though some of the inventions came about a long time ago, accessible mass-produced entertainment is pretty new—no more than 300 or so years old. Just look at popular music: in a very short time we've gone from people only hearing music when it was performed live, to the norm being record players you had to crank by hand, to tape machines, CD players, and now MP3s and other kinds of digital files. As technology makes new things possible, pop culture changes. But the core elements—its accessibility, availability, and ability to create an experience/emotion—always remain the same whether you're listening to

This Seems... Familiar:
A Quick Look at Genre

GENRE IS WHAT makes the mainstream pop culture we spend so much time with instantly familiar to us.

Basically, a genre is a recognizable type of corporate pop culture. In movies, the different genres include action/adventure, comedy, romance, drama, and horror. In television, the genres are similar, but they get even more specific: sitcom (comedy), soap opera (drama), science fiction (action/adventure), cop show (drama–action/adventure). Music has genres including rap, pop, rock, and punk, and, within each of these, ever more specific categories that, at a certain point, start to seem kinda ridiculous. (You ever wonder what the difference is between rock, pop, post-rock, rockabilly, and punk rock?)

Each genre comes with a particular feel, look, and pace—so much so that if I were to show you a five-minute clip from a movie or television show you've never seen before, even with the sound muted you would probably be able to say what genre it belongs to.

Genres came about largely so that it would be easier to market certain kinds of products to certain specific audiences. So, romantic comedies are marketed to women. Horror movies are marketed to teenagers. Punk music to angry college kids. Sitcoms to young adults in their twenties and thirties. Dramas and soap operas to women in their thirties and forties. The idea behind genre is that if you can say who exactly the target market for the pop product is, then you can easily focus your marketing and promotion efforts on those people.

When making our own DIY entertainment, genre is something that limits our creativity; in other words, its rules are not to be respected. You're far better off making whatever music you want than worrying if you are correctly following the rules for deep house, club house, disco house, or techno house. Throughout the history of pop culture, great independent creators have brought styles, sounds, and looks together. Often their success has involved merging different things we are familiar with into something completely new.

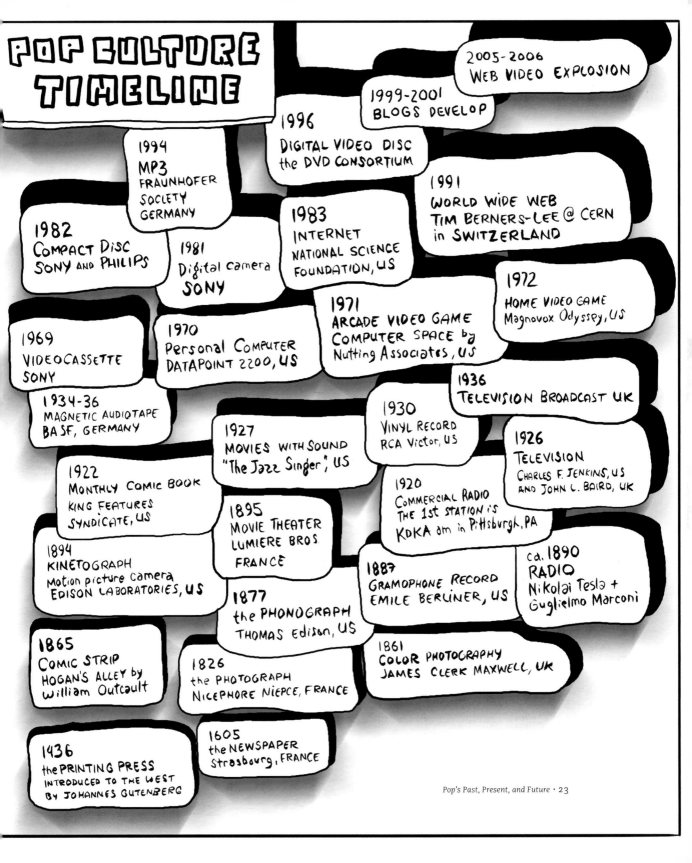

POP CULTURE TIMELINE

2005-2006 WEB VIDEO EXPLOSION

1999-2001 BLOGS DEVELOP

1996 DIGITAL VIDEO DISC the DVD CONSORTIUM

1994 MP3 FRAUNHOFER SOCIETY GERMANY

1991 WORLD WIDE WEB TIM BERNERS-LEE @ CERN in SWITZERLAND

1983 INTERNET NATIONAL SCIENCE FOUNDATION, US

1982 COMPACT DISC SONY AND PHILIPS

1981 Digital camera SONY

1972 HOME VIDEO GAME Magnovox Odyssey, US

1971 ARCADE VIDEO GAME COMPUTER SPACE by Nutting Associates, US

1970 Personal Computer DATAPOINT 2200, US

1969 VIDEOCASSETTE SONY

1936 TELEVISION BROADCAST UK

1934-36 MAGNETIC AUDIOTAPE BASF, GERMANY

1930 VINYL RECORD RCA Victor, US

1927 MOVIES WITH SOUND "The Jazz Singer", US

1926 TELEVISION CHARLES F. JENKINS, US AND JOHN L. BAIRD, UK

1922 MONTHLY COMIC BOOK KING FEATURES SYNDICATE, US

1920 COMMERCIAL RADIO THE 1st STATION is KDKA am in Pittsburgh, PA

1895 MOVIE THEATER LUMIERE BROS. FRANCE

1894 KINETOGRAPH Motion picture camera EDISON LABORATORIES, US

1887 GRAMOPHONE RECORD EMILE BERLINER, US

ca.1890 RADIO Nikolai Tesla + Guglielmo Marconi

1877 the PHONOGRAPH THOMAS Edison, US

1865 Comic STRIP HOGAN'S ALLEY by William Outcault

1861 COLOR PHOTOGRAPHY JAMES CLERK MAXWELL, UK

1826 the PHOTOGRAPH NICEPHORE NIEPCE, FRANCE

1605 the NEWSPAPER Strasbourg, FRANCE

1436 the PRINTING PRESS INTRODUCED TO THE WEST BY JOHANNES GUTENBERG

These guys may not look like pop culture pioneers, but Gutenberg's movable type led to a renaissance of learning, as well as a revolution—the scientific one.

It's easy to look around at all the fast-paced, thrilling diversions we have at our disposal and assume that entertainment is pretty new, something developed just for us. But there has always been entertainment in our societies, and at any given time people have probably thought that what they were doing for fun was just about the greatest thing since cooking meat with fire.

Okay, so it wasn't always fast-paced action. But different societies had their equivalent of going to the movies (storytelling circles), heading out for a night at the club (ritual dances), and even playing video games (leading the young on a fake hunt). Songs and dances and stories were ways to teach young people how to do everything from respect their elders to go on dates. At a time when people lived off the land and depended on each other for their survival, culture offered not only a way to relax and celebrate life, but also opportunities to teach young people the rules of their society.

music on the long-extinct eight-track or on your cell phone.

Stories without Pretty Pictures

This kind of culture was made accessible and popular because of the way it was handed down from person to person, from generation to generation, as different stories, lessons, dances, songs, and other activities circulated through families and small communities. Stories were do-it-yourself entertainment in a time before electricity and mass production. This was the beginning of pop culture. The original folktales were popular, accessible, and reproduced over and over again—not in the factory, of course, but by people passing the stories around to each other.

Folk is the Future?

Folk. You're probably thinking some guy with an acoustic guitar droning on about rain and wheat. But folk music got its name when there were only acoustic (non-electric) instruments, which were played by local people to entertain everyone else. Think of the band that led the square dance or the village women putting on a traditional dance.

Folk comes from the German word *volk*, which means "people." Passed on from generation to generation, folk culture is what some think of as "natural" culture, a culture that wasn't created by experts and then churned out in distant factories, but was made by "the people" right in their com-

Is this what "folk" means to you? The days when we eagerly awaited family concerts featuring cousin Franz on the accordion are over.

munities and homes. You *buy* pop culture, which is produced by experts in places like Hollywood. You *make* folk culture, which is produced by you and sis jamming on homespun banjos.

Folk culture sounds kinda dull, and hey, let's face it—anyone who's ever been stuck listening to their relatives wail away on the piano knows there's something to be said for having more choice in how you spend your evenings. All the same, folk culture teaches us that human beings weren't meant to sit silent and motionless in front of a screen while someone else tells us a story. History shows us that people have always entertained each other, told each other stories, danced with each other, sung songs together. Many believe that for human beings to be truly happy and healthy, we need to get back to having a shared culture that we can all be part of. Even if it does mean losing some of the glitz.

The Rise of the Professional Entertainer

Around 200 years ago, folk culture started to change into pop culture. With the invention of the steam engine and electricity and all the good stuff they call the Industrial Revolution (which meant the arrival of "industry," a.k.a. factories churning out tons of cheap product), people changed the way they lived their lives. They began working in factories and offices and spent less time together

hunting buffalo or bringing in the crops—the sorts of group activities that were often done while singing the popular tune of the time or retelling an old folk story. In other words, people had fewer reasons to get together and share stories. Everyone was becoming a specialist, doing a particular job over and over again instead of farming, hunting, making clothes, shaping pottery, and telling that special favorite story about the mermaid.

So, to get to the point, one of the things that all these new specialized factory and office workers started buying was entertainment. They were happy to pay an expert performer to tell them jokes or sing them songs, because it was quicker and easier than doing it themselves. When they got home from work, they were too tired to tell stories, and anyway, they had money now—they could go out and buy their stories.

Professional entertainers began to emerge. These were people who traveled from town to town to tell popular stories, sing songs, or act out plays. Early specialists were mostly theater troupes. Naturally, these actors and singers and dancers and magicians all expected to be paid for their efforts. And because they were specialists

Published by **Kunkel Brothers** N19 N. Fifth St
Mammoth Music House

Traveling troupes like this band of minstrels (from the late 1800s) were gradually replaced by recorded music. Factory workers (below) assemble jukeboxes, which were the first form of sound recording for the public. Then came mass-produced records, tapes, CDs, iPods...

getting paid, the audience demanded a higher standard of entertainment than you would get if your neighbor was performing. It's like the difference between asking a friend how to cure your flu and going to see a real doctor.

So we start to see the kind of pop culture we know today shaping up. This is a culture in which experts tell audiences stories and sing songs. Today we don't even usually go out and see the traveling storytellers, musicians, and theater troupes that come through our city or town, but more often than not we stay home and watch them on TV or hear their music on the radio.

One Big Family: Pop Culture Goes Global

Specialists started making "popular" culture as a job. And in order to make more money, they figured out ways to standardize their performances, which meant they pretty much did the same shtick over and over again. Think of any popular band on tour. You don't figure they are going to do a completely different performance in all 50 stadiums, do you? Of course not. They are going to play the same songs every time.

Gradually, people became so used to getting a great show that they forgot how to entertain themselves, and a lot of unique cultures started being forgotten. The people in those cultures weren't passing on their stories, dances, folktales, recipes, and even languages because they were too busy working and making money. And the professionals they hired to entertain them were only going to use bits and pieces of community-based, older folk cultures so that their material wasn't too local and they could tell the same story to different people wherever they went.

Today there are folk cultures that are slowly dying out and will soon be forgotten completely. At the same time, the rise of pop culture means that more and more people have quick and easy access to all kinds of fun pastimes, whether we're talking about cable TV, theme parks, or songs on the radio. We no longer have to wait for the once-a-month village hoedown or the

after-the-barn-raising storytelling to get our entertainment. With pop culture being mass produced, we have access to the millions of movies, pop songs, and video games made all over the world by experts whose job it is to make sure these entertainments are fun and affordable.

In previous societies, culture and entertainment and leisure were all wrapped up in everyday life. Today, we expect our entertainment time and our work time to be different. We don't go to church to be entertained and we don't have amateur hour at our relatives' weddings. We have, instead, blocks of leisure time we want to fill—after school, on the weekends—without necessarily lifting a finger.

Most of us fill our leisure time with the products that contain pop culture (books, DVDs, websites, CD-ROMs). And today we are all turning to the same sources for entertainment as one huge group of users. The ability of pop culture to make us all feel like we are part of one global family is mass-produced entertainment's biggest achievement.

The Cinderella Theme

Because so many people all experience the same bunch of products, pop culture has the ability to introduce powerful messages into societies all over the world. One of the great universal messages of pop culture is that people should pursue their dreams. Again and again, pop culture reminds us that we are capable of anything we set our mind to. Many of our most beloved, popular stories are based on the fairy tale of Cinderella, which emerged, originally, from folk culture. You know the story, of course: a princess reduced to cleaning up after her evil stepsisters, Cinderella is eventually discovered by a handsome prince and rescued from her life of servitude. It boils down to a plot that we are now very familiar with—the poor person who is treated badly through no fault of his or her own but is finally rescued into a life of happiness and luxury.

It's difficult to say exactly when or how this story came to be the central message of pop culture. But we can say for sure that the early days of pop culture were also the early days of advertising and marketing. Advertisements in the 18th and 19th centuries focused on the product for sale. An ad might say: *These gloves are really comfortable and will keep your hands warm.* But by the early 20th century, the pitch had changed. We were being told (as we are still being told today): *These gloves will make you feel sexy and hip and popular.* Pop culture and advertising fed off each other. People who were just figuring out how to make magazines and movies were learning that to capture people's attention it was best to focus on the individual—how each person could change, could become, say, rich, famous, or beautiful. So, as pop culture evolved from the folk culture of Cinderella, the theme and even the story stayed the same, but the characters weren't princes and princesses anymore: they were you and me.

Forget talking mirrors, witches, spells, and pumpkins turning into carriages. Pop culture is wildly successful by bringing fantasy into everyday reality and making what happens to the main character seem like something that could happen to us one day. Which is why we see a lot of movies like *Maid in Manhattan* and *Pretty Woman*, TV dramas like *Charmed*, *Sabrina the Teenage Witch*, and *Smallville*, and reality shows like *American Idol*, *The Bachelor*, and *The Apprentice*. This is Cinderella all over again, isn't it? Over and over, it's ordinary people "transformed" into something better, whether through convincing a business mogul to make them their apprentice or learning to use their powers as a teenage witch or superhero.

The ultimate effect is a steady barrage of stories that tell us that, no matter who we are, we can achieve more. This encourages millions around the world to pursue careers and possibilities they would otherwise consider far beyond them. It also encourages people to stand up for their rights and demand equal treatment in society. If we all believe that we can do better and that we deserve better, then we are less likely to be pushovers. This is pop culture's gift to us. At the same time, though, pop culture's universal theme seems to be "you're special, you deserve more." People feel entitled to fame and fortune, and cheated because they don't have the jewels, mansions, and sports cars of celebrities. This desire for fame and attention leads to a sense of dissatisfaction with ordinary, everyday life. Why study hard, be honest, care about your

JOHN ROBINSONS 10 BIG SHOWS COMBINED

THE MEETING OF KING SOLOMON AND THE QUEEN OF SHEBA.

WITH THE MAGNIFICENT SPECTACLE KING SOLOMON HIS TEMPLE AND THE QUEEN OF SHEBA

Circus shows attracted audiences with acrobats, wild animals, freaks, and the lure of immorality. This act in 1899 featured the fictional African king Solomon, surrounded by dancing girls—scandalous!

friends and community, when you're going to be a famous rap star? Almost since the emergence of pop culture, critics have wondered if this new mass entertainment medium is turning people against everyday life and community values.

Recent History: Pop Culture as Moral Panic

As pop culture began to replace folk culture, more and more people became concerned about the messages pop culture was putting into society. After all, it encouraged everyone to do what they felt like rather than what they were told. Pop culture told people they deserved more out of life. Elders, religious leaders, even governments started worrying that pop culture was a bad influence—its focus was on in-your-face entertainment rather than education or community values. Even things like traveling circuses were viewed as a dangerous form of entertainment from their beginnings in the 1700s. To convince people that circuses were not morally evil, animal displays and acts had to be included so that the circuses could claim their shows were "educational." Even with ani-

mals, circuses continued to be viewed by many as immoral entertainment that taught children and adolescents and impressionable adults the wrong kinds of behavior.

In the 1940s and 1950s, both the Canadian Parliament and the Congress of the United States started to worry that horror comics with titles like *Tales from the Crypt* were corrupting young people. Canada actually banned horror comics in 1948. Meanwhile, the U.S. Congress called in witnesses and eventually the comic companies agreed to censor themselves, a move that resulted in many of them going broke and a virtual end to the popular horror comics of the time.

In the 1950s and 1960s, as rock music was emerging as a force in popular culture, there was much talk about it being evil, even a product of the devil. Critics pointed to Elvis Presley and the hordes of young people who admired him as proof that rock and roll was bad. In a famous incident, when Presley performed on a popular variety TV show, public pressure forced the producers to film him from the waist up because it was feared his gyrating dance moves—he was known at the time as "Elvis the pelvis"—would be corrupting.

It's fiction, honest. The radio production of sci-fi fable *War of the Worlds* by H.G. Wells (pictured here) was so convincing that people fled from the "alien invasion," despite frequent reminders that it was only a dramatization.

Governments have generally responded to the shift from community folk culture to pop culture by introducing various forms of ratings and restrictions. Teenagers are banned from seeing certain kinds of movies until they are 16 or 18. There are also restrictions on video games and even music. Some have argued that these restrictions are basically a form of censorship. Others feel that young people in society need to be protected from certain ideas and images until they are mature enough to understand what they are seeing.

Reality: Uncensored

Today pop culture is the main way we get stories and information about our society. So it's no wonder that so many people are worried about what pop culture is saying. Our entertainments mostly show people with perfectly toned slim bodies, expert makeup, and great outfits. But what pop culture *says*—like the lessons we learn in school and at home—is that it doesn't matter what we look like, it's what we are like *inside* that counts. All those successful, rich beauty queens and muscle-bound hunks on TV seem to contradict everything we are being taught.

All the same, we have to remember: *pop culture is not folk culture.* We are no longer dependent on

culture to teach us what is important for survival in our community. That is, after all, why we have all those teachers, priests, police officers, and doctors. Pop culture developed into a specialized field meant first and foremost to entertain. But because so much of pop culture is still tied up with folk culture—scary movies are often just fancy versions of "Hansel and Gretel"—there remains a lot of confusion regarding the role of pop in society. There are those who insist that any kind of mass entertainment which isn't educational is bad. They figure that pop culture which doesn't have a good moral is probably destroying society. But this is mostly a hangover from previous eras, when folk culture was a necessary part of educating the younger generation.

So when we hear about how pop culture is ruining lives and destroying civilization, well, I'd be a bit skeptical. Don't believe the hype! Remember that over the years people have got upset over everything from Elvis to horror comic books to Madonna to shock rocker Marilyn Manson (once banned from performing by some towns and

POP CULTURE hysteria through the decades

1938 A radio production of the H.G. Wells story *War of the Worlds* causes thousands in the U.S. to believe that the earth has been invaded by Martians who are in the process of trashing New York and New Jersey.

1954 Psychologist Frederic Wertham publishes *A Seduction of Innocents*, a book which claims that comic books are corrupting youth. This prompts the United States Congress to order the comics industry to police itself, and results in the Comics Code Authority. The popular horror comics genre all but disappears.

1957 The publication of *Howl and Other Poems* by Allen Ginsberg leads to the arrest of the book's publisher, poet Lawrence Ferlinghetti, as well as the City Lights bookstore manager Shigeyoshi Murao on charges of selling obscene material. A judge, also a Sunday school Bible teacher, finds them not guilty later that year.

1964 The Kingsmen's song "Louie Louie" is banned in Indiana after reports that, if you play the record at the wrong speed, secret "dirty lyrics" are audible.

1966 The John Lennon comment that the Beatles are more popular than Jesus results in widespread record burnings and protests.

1971 Stanley Kubrick voluntarily withdraws his film *A Clockwork Orange* from release in Europe after fears that it is causing moviegoers to riot and rape. The film does not get shown again in movie theaters in the United Kingdom until 2000.

1972 Radio stations ban John Denver's song "Rocky Mountain High," fearing the word "high" refers to a drug-induced state.

1985 Tipper Gore and other wives of prominent Washington politicians successfully lobby for parental warning stickers that will be placed on all recordings containing graphic depictions of sex and/or violence. Many stores refuse to sell any recording that has the sticker on it.

1996 Wal-Mart refuses to carry Sheryl Crow's self-titled second album because one of the songs contains an unflattering comment about the discount retailer's gun sales policy.

1999 High school students at Kettle Moraine High School in Wales, Wisconsin, must be 18 or older to read *Rolling Stone* magazine at the school library, even though a child of any age can buy the mag at local stores.

2005 Senator Hillary Clinton announces plans to introduce legislation to crack down on inappropriate material in video games after Grand Theft Auto is shown to be easily modified to reveal scenes of simulated sex.

Culture is basically a conversation between people, but right now it usually feels like the conversation is going one way. Corporations and celebrities talk—we listen.

governments) to rapper Eminem. It's easy to say that the solution is to censor or ban parts of pop culture, but this is rarely successful. When I was 12, I really wanted to see horror movies like *Friday the 13th*. Because they were rated R, I figured those movies must be full of *really* interesting adult stuff, and I did everything I could think of to sneak into one. The point is, we are always most interested in those things we are told we can't have. Today, I can't really remember what I thought was so great about all those movies with blood spattering everywhere and bad actors pretending to be scared.

The real problem with pop culture is not that it is immoral; it's that we don't really get a say in what gets beamed into our houses and brains. Yes, pop culture is too devoted to using violence and sex to get our attention. But mass entertainment doesn't have to be like that. This is what happens when pop becomes more about selling a product than about helping people to communicate with each other.

It's time for a change. It's our turn to talk. The future of pop culture is a shift back to its origins as a folk culture: a culture that is about everyone sharing their ideas and stories and emotions. If we don't like what we are seeing on television or what someone is singing about in a rap song, then what we need is the knowledge and tools to speak back and put out a different message.

There are problems with the way our culture works, but that doesn't mean we have to throw our televisions out the window and burn our iPods. The answer is not to plunge ourselves into silence, but to be able to change the channel to something we do like—maybe even something we made ourselves.

Further Reading

Encyclopedia of American Social History
by Peter Williams

Mondo Canuck: A Canadian Pop Culture Odyssey
by Geoff Pevere and Greig Dymond

Popular Culture: A User's Guide by Imre Szeman
and Susie O'Brien

St. James Encyclopedia of Popular Culture
edited by Tom and Sara Pendergast

*Taboo Tunes: A History of Banned Bands and Censored
Songs* by Peter Blecha

Do It Yourself

GRANDPA, WHAT'S A RECORD PLAYER? Interview
your grandparents or other members of the generation before television. Ask them what they used
to do for fun when they were teenagers, in an age
before video games, cable, and online chat.

TV TURN-OFF WEEKEND Invite your friends and
family to join you in spending a weekend without pop! No television, no Internet, no music, no
video games. Write up an hourly log of how you
keep yourself entertained. Harder than it sounds,
isn't it?

EVERYTHING OLD IS NEW AGAIN Much of what
we think is original and new in pop culture is
really borrowed from the folk culture and fairy
tales of the past. Make an old/new list and keep
adding to it every time you see something that's
just a copy. Old: Cinderella. New: *Pretty Woman*;
Maid in Manhattan. Old: Hansel and Gretel. New:
The Blair Witch Project.

DEFINING YOURSELF Make a video, write a song,
draw a comic, or do up a zine that defines "popular culture" in five minutes or less. Good luck!

Keyword Search

pop culture (history of)

folk culture

censorship

mass culture (history of, technology)

genre

Attack of the Blob!

Pop Culture Everywhere

Revenge of the Dark Side

In the United States, Hollywood industry statistics tell us that some 37,500 movie screens feature about 500 movies a year. Which means that 500 movies a year tell the stories of a population of 300 million people. So what I'm wondering is: if only 500 people get to have their movies shown, what happens to everyone else who wants to make a movie? It would seem that they are out of luck.

According to media reports on the movie industry, the average cost of producing and marketing each of those 500 movies is around $89 million. When you are competing with Hollywood studios that not only own the cinema chains but also spend millions making sure that their product looks great and everybody knows about it, there's not much chance that your movie is going to be in a theater near you anytime soon.

Things don't look much better for those hoping to get a song on the radio. An article in the online magazine *Salon* notes that Clear Channel corporation owns 1,200 radio stations in America,

more than half of all the rock/pop stations in the market. With a single head office deciding what will be played on these stations, getting your song on their playlist is big business. And according to the *New York Times*, record companies pay anywhere from $250,000 to $1 million to market a song as a good pick for play on top 40 radio.

Planning on publishing a new magazine and getting it into stores? Good luck. The *New York Times* reports that just four companies control 90 percent of the business of distributing magazines, which means that your mag is only going to get on the rack if one of those four companies thinks it's going to sell thousands of copies. (And unless your magazine features a skimpily clad celebrity on the cover, it's probably never going to.)

So let me get this straight, you're thinking: I can make a movie but can't get it into the theaters, I can record songs but won't hear them on the radio, and I can publish a magazine but shouldn't expect to see it at the 7-Eleven next to the nacho chips in the foreseeable future.

Well, hate to break it to you, but that is pretty much the situation. Distribution of pop culture is almost totally controlled by a handful of media companies. Those companies, which own smaller companies all around the world, get to decide everything from what's on TV to what's in the newspaper.

Slings and Arrows of Outrageous Fortune: The Two Kinds of Pop Culture

So...you're now thinking...not much point reading this book, then, is there?

Well, yes and no. It depends on what you're hoping to achieve. Just because you can't reach the same audience that Steven Spielberg and Jennifer Lopez can doesn't mean that you shouldn't be making your own pop culture. After all, shouldn't everyone have a chance to tell their story? Isn't that what pop culture is all about? The purpose of this book is, in many ways, to fight against the way these corporations have turned pop culture into a for-profit pursuit that prevents ordinary people like you and me from being part of it. We need more ways to speak to each other without having to beg to have our story turned into a product by some giant company. By making your own pop culture, you are, in your own little way, challenging the corporate monopoly and changing the world.

Take a look at the drawing on page 39. It shows the two different forms of pop culture. I call them "corporate" pop culture and "independent" pop culture.

Corporate pop culture is represented by an arrow pointing one way: straight down. We're pretty familiar with corporate pop culture—it's *Shrek* the movie, Shrek the kiddie meal at Burger King, Shrek the video game, *Shrek* the DVD with exciting bonus features. Corporate pop culture is top-down culture. This means that a few people at the top decide what kind of stories will be told and which products will be sold to the rest of us waiting at the bottom.

As you can see, "independent" pop culture is an arrow moving across the page and pointing in both directions. That's because independent culture moves from person to person. There's room for a lot more voices. Anyone can make independent culture—including you. Independent culture doesn't depend on snappy marketing campaigns with giant billboards, ads in newspapers, or fancy websites. It depends on friends and communities.

In other words, you do a zine, pass it around to your friends, send some to people in other cities, and leave some for sale at the local record store. Your ideas get out there slowly and by word of mouth. *Hey, you've got to see my friend Allison's zine—she obsesses over her boyfriend, claims to have invented the tofu sloppy joe, and has a comic about failing a math test. Check it out. You'll like it.*

Independent pop culture spreads slowly. It is less likely to make any one person rich and famous. But it gives more people the opportunity to tell stories, talk about their lives, and express what they think.

Hop on the Assembly Line: Exploring the Inner Machine of Corporate Pop Culture

But for now, corporate pop culture dominates our society. Corporate pop culture is the pop you know best, because you see it every day. It's what you get on TV, on movie screens, at the video store, on the radio. Corporations make our video games and publish our magazines. Often we don't even realize how much of what gets beamed into our brains emerges from giant companies with branches all over the world. Studies have shown that the aver-age North American watches four hours of television daily; and the majority of the programs we watch are made by companies owned by shareholders whose main concern is profit.

When a company makes a movie, or a video game, or a CD, there are all kinds of technicians and experts who are involved and employed. Millions of dollars are spent on everything from costumes to graphics to editing to marketing the product. When we watch television (or take in a movie, or flip through an entertainment maga-zine), we just see the finished project, so slick and enticing that it often feels as if it has come from another world.

The look of pop culture is deliberate, of course. The cooler the product appears, the more people will want to check it out. And corporations are always desperate to get people excited about the latest, greatest entertainment. They have to earn back hundreds of millions of dollars, after all. Which is why a new movie's advertising campaign is everywhere—on TV, on billboards, in magazines, even on cereal boxes and toys.

That's pretty much how most of the pop culture we see every day operates. When it works, it can be wildly successful. According to Hollywood

industry media reports, *Star Wars: Revenge of the Sith* cost $115 million to make, but the studio took in around $850 million. And that doesn't include DVD sales and spin-offs such as toys, T-shirts, posters, and video games. Of course, sometimes corporate pop culture stumbles by backing an entertainment that doesn't find a big enough audience. For instance, a movie epic based on the ancient warrior Alexander was a flop, costing $150 million to make and earning the studio only around $70 million at the box office. But don't feel bad: Warner Brothers isn't going broke anytime soon.

Made You Buy

Have you ever wanted to have the hair of a pop star or the car of the latest James Bond? You're not the only one. In her book *The Overspent American*, Juliet Schor argues that the more we are exposed to the lifestyles of the rich and famous, the more we want to look and live like them— which often means buying the expensive clothes and accessories.

Corporate pop culture is full of products you can buy. Movies and TV shows sell the rights for products to appear onscreen to the highest bidder. This isn't just the trailers and ads before the feature: it's the sunglasses the starlet wears while she blows away those who threaten world freedom. Ever since the movie E.T. *The Extraterrestrial* featured an alien addicted to Reese's Pieces, *product placement* has been the norm. Is it any wonder Schor's study found that the more television we watch, the more money we spend? We don't just want the star's outfit, we also want the star's character's outfit. "While our real-life friends still matter," writes Schor, "they have been joined by our media 'friends.' We watch the way television families live, we read about the lifestyles of celebrities and other public figures we admire, and we consciously and unconsciously assimilate this information."

Corporate pop culture makes it easy to be entertained without having to do too much. If you're bored, you can just switch on the TV or

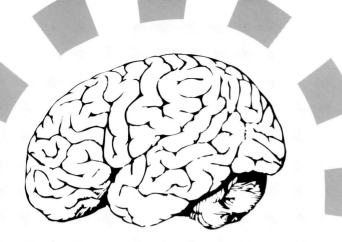

pop in a video game or watch a movie. We all do it. We visit websites to play the free games, we travel to theme parks and go on cool rides like the Spider-man 3-D roller coaster at Florida's Universal Studios, we watch TV shows, rent videos, download music—we are entertained 365 days a year.

Some of the things we do are quite expensive—like special trips to theme parks—but others, such as watching TV or listening to the radio or visiting websites, are either free or really cheap. Click that mouse or remote control and away you go!

Another good thing about corporate pop culture is that it is professionally done. Generally, with this kind of entertainment, you know that it will be engaging and exciting. The special effects make the movies look real (however fantastic they are!), the photos in the magazine are luscious and colorful, the actors on TV are convincingly funny or sad, the video games make you feel that you really are engaged in a massive space battle.

But there's bad news, too. The bad news is that corporate pop culture is everywhere. Wait a minute, you're thinking—that's the same as the good news. Well, exactly. When one kind of thing is everywhere, it tends to force out everything else. The kind of pop culture that corporations make is like that horror-movie blob, a science experiment which, once released, slowly but surely eats everything and everyone until there's nothing else left.

THEY EAT YOUR BRAINS!
Five Biggest and What They Own
(and this isn't even everything . . .)

AOL/TIME-WARNER
MAGAZINES: more than 60, including *Time*, *Life*, and *People*
MOVIES: Warner Brothers, New Line, and Fine Line
MUSIC: Warner Brothers, Atlantic, Elektra
TV: CNN, WB Network, Cartoon Network, HBO
BOOKS: Little, Brown Publishing
INTERNET: America Online

DISNEY
MOVIES: Disney/Buena Vista Pictures, Miramax, Touchstone
TV: ABC, Disney Channel, Discover, ESPN, A&E, Biography
BOOKS: Hyperion Publishing

MURDOCH'S NEWS CORPORATION
MOVIES: 20th Century Fox, Fox Searchlight
TV: Fox Network, National Geographic, Golf Channel
BOOKS: HarperCollins Publishers
INTERNET: MySpace, IGN

BERTELSMANN
MUSIC: BMG, Arista
BOOKS: Random House, Knopf, Doubleday

VIACOM
MOVIES: Paramount Pictures, Blockbuster
TV: CBS, MTV, Nickelodeon, UPN, TNN, The Movie Channel, BET
BOOKS: Simon & Schuster
INTERNET: iFilm, goCityKids, Neopets, Gametrailers

Great Lemonade... Till Your Teeth Fall Out

Remember, corporate pop culture is created to earn investors and owners money. That is the first priority. And the most money is made when a lot of people are enticed to all buy the same thing. So a big goal of corporate pop culture is to keep its audience away from other kinds of cultural expression. As you can see in the sidebar on page 41, a handful of companies make the bulk of our entertainment, and they are very successful at keeping everything else off the TV, off the big screen, out of the video store, out of magazines and newspapers, and generally out of our field of vision altogether.

That, in the end, is the biggest problem with corporate pop culture: it sells culture to us as if it's a giant lemonade factory producing a drink that's cheap and sweet. This lemonade, like a lot of our favorite sugary carbonated beverages, tastes really good the first time, so good that we keep wanting more. But in the long run, the sugary syrup from the factory gives us rotten teeth, makes us fat, and, worst of all, makes us forget that we can create our own lemonade with tap water, lemon juice, and sugar. Because the mass-produced stuff is so tasty and easy to get, people who want to open a tiny stand next to the factory to sell something else—say, fresh-squeezed juice—find that no one is interested. Why should I drink your expensive juice when I can buy a gallon of this delicious sweet lemonade for the same price? And anyway, your juice tastes weird compared with the lemonade—are you sure you're using enough sugar?

Revenge of the Kids: Independent Pop Culture

Independent pop culture is the juice stand next to the giant lemonade factory. In many ways, it works the same as corporate entertainment. The intent is to make pop culture—to make movies, or songs,

Joe Ollman's comic collection *Wag* came to fruition after many years of building up a loyal audience for his self-published comic zines.

or video games, or entertainment magazines and websites, that other people will want to see. The focus, then, is on turning an idea into a mass-produced "product" that can reach an audience.

But there are also big differences between independent pop culture and corporate pop culture. First of all, indie pop culture is individual and/or community based. In indie pop culture, if you want to make a movie or sing a song or put out a magazine, you just go out and do it. And it's done by individuals and collectives who are usually very passionate about getting a certain story or message or feeling out into the world. They may still sell their music or charge admission to their movie, but making a huge profit is not their goal.

Say, for instance, you are someone who has always really loved animal movies, books, and stories. Yes, you are that rare breed—a really big fan of Lassie, the Black Stallion, Willy the Dolphin, and Babe the pig. Now, you can spend all your time waiting for the next animal movie or TV show to appear, or you can decide to share your love of animal stories with the world. Maybe you start a zine or a website. The next thing you know, you're writing your own animal story.

Maybe you still don't see the difference between indie and corporate production. After all, a talking animal story is a talking animal story, right? Which is, in a way, my point. There have

been talking animal stories all throughout history. This is a big part of our folk culture. Suddenly, though, it seems as if only a handful of scriptwriters get to tell these stories to the world.

Many of us have never even seen an independently created movie or TV show or magazine. But believe it or not, there are lots of people doing this stuff. All over the world, people are making their own movies, TV shows, music, websites, video games, magazines, and radio shows. You probably know people who have a website dedicated to, say, their cat or their favorite pop star, or even to themselves in the form of a blog. Or maybe you know someone who has recorded some songs and burned a bunch of CD-ROMS on computer to hand

PEDDLING COOL

COOL IS JUST another way to get you addicted to buying stuff—what's cool, who's cool, how can I be cool? It's all nonsense. The whole idea of cool, along with words like *hip* and *edgy*, is essentially a marketing campaign for corporate pop culture. Companies spend a lot of money trying to get people to think a certain band, outfit, movie, or cell phone is cool, and a lot of this money is directed at teens. A company might give away a product to a bunch of young people they think are trendsetters, in the hope that the rest of us losers, desperate to be cool, will see the stylish kids using the product and go out and buy it. Pop culture corporations have also been known to conduct guerrilla graffiti campaigns in which they hire teens to do graffiti and put up posters and stickers for certain bands or movies. This is supposed to look spontaneous and "street" (the epitome of cool) and make people think that a certain band really has the support of the local community. The goal at the end of the day is to keep young people interested in constantly buying new fashions, accessories, and entertainment products. As in: It's so not cool to still be listening to that band. As in: What do you mean you haven't seen it? Are you some kind of loser? Those who want to make their own music or movies and don't care about having the newest pair of $300 sneakers are, in this scheme, losers. But the next time someone accuses you of not being cool enough, remember this: the coolest people never think about being cool.

VINAY MENON IS a TV critic. He spends all his time watching and writing about corporate television. Now it's time for him to explain himself!

You work as a TV critic for the Toronto Star, *a major daily newspaper. A lot of people think they could be TV critics. What makes you the right person for the job?*

In some ways, I think we're all TV critics. But when it comes to writing a column, you have to do more than just watch. For example, it's not unusual for me to spend up to 12 hours a day reviewing tapes, researching, interviewing, and writing. Even though it's TV, I approach it like any other serious beat.

TV shows are always being criticized. Are the shows really as bad as people claim?

Yes and no. Overall, TV has improved over the past five years. But television has a bad reputation it can't shake. With an explosion in the number of shows, the gap between "good" and "bad" seems to expand each season. In turn, this makes the bad seem worse than it probably is.

Why don't more ordinary, everyday people have opportunities to be on TV?

When *Survivor* premiered in 2000, many thought it would unleash a wave of new opportunities. But so-called reality TV has become just another avenue for aspiring Hollywood stars. Until the U.S. networks find a way to make money with everyday citizens, most of us will be excluded.

What do you love most about watching television?

I am a big fan of television. In fact, I nearly turned down this job because I never wanted TV to feel like work. At its best, television makes me forget everything in the world. But, strangely, it also makes me feel connected to the world. You can't ask for more.

Any advice for young people who want to create their own television shows outside of the corporate system?

Technology has changed so much in the past decade. Now, with a digital video camera, some software, and creative vision, anybody can produce content. Think of an interesting story and decide how you want to tell it. Show it to your friends. Maybe put it online. Never get frustrated with corporate roadblocks. If you're good, they'll eventually notice.

out to friends. Someone might do a zine and leave it lying around coffee shops and record stores or hand it out at school.

Independent pop culture takes many different forms, and is often inspired and influenced by the for-profit entertainment put out by big companies. But the important thing to remember is that it is spontaneous and part of a community. You don't have to be an expert, and you don't have to have a degree in cinematography or a lot of fancy equipment. Most importantly, you don't have to get permission from a group of bosses whose responsibility is to make sure they are investing money in something that will sell. You can just get out there and write and publish and promote your story, which means you get to say what you think and feel.

Indie culture – selling out or buying in?

It would be a big mistake to think that all corporate pop culture is bad and all independent pop culture is good. The fact is, there is lots of corporate pop culture that is really good, and lots of independent pop culture that is really bad. Ultimately it is up to you and me to decide whether that talking animal story featuring a rattlesnake who falls in love with a polar bear is quality entertainment worthy of our time. At the end of the day, nobody can tell you what is right or wrong about

your work. If you make something that only a few people like, that's fine—so long as you are happy with what you've achieved.

A lot of not-so-good independent pop culture happens when people are trying to imitate what they see on TV or hear on the radio. Desperate to be singers and actors, people can lose sight of reality. They dream of being exactly like the performers they see every day because that's the only kind of entertainment they know. So, when they make indie pop culture, they try to imitate the big-budget stuff. While this isn't necessarily bad—many great artists got their start imitating their heroes—it's not exactly what I have in mind when I picture people making their own indie pop.

Sometimes people make indie products that get bought up by the big corporations. Things get confusing when you think about, say, someone making a movie on their own and then having it bought by a big studio. This is relatively rare, but it does happen, such as in the case of the indie documentary *Supersize Me.* Audiences responded so well to this movie about the dangers of eating too much fast food that it was picked up by a big studio for major distribution across North America. So there *are* weird hybrid situations in which a corporation buys up something that started as an indie project. When this happens, we have to wonder: is the project still indie? As always, nothing is fixed in stone. Pop culture in general

HOW MUCH INDIE CULTURE IS OUT THERE?

IT'S HARD TO say because, unlike corporations that record every sale, the world of indie culture is impossible to keep track of. New ideas come and go very quickly. But it's fair to say that the numbers are growing fast based on the statistics we do have:

★ According to published reports, there are an estimated 5 million bloggers in North America.

★ A *New York Times* article suggests that roughly 35 percent of the average recording studio's income comes from people recording their own music (and that doesn't take into account those recording on home equipment in their basement).

★ Published market research studies show that sales of home video recording equipment are worth billions of dollars and continue to grow.

★ Online searches show that there are thousands of independent magazines and zines published in both online and print formats in North America.

★ Online searches also show that thousands of people are running their own web radio stations online.

So how much indie culture is out there? Well . . . more than any one of us knows about, that's for sure!

Staying Free!

STAY FREE!

PRANKS ISSUE

STAY FREE IS a zine in New York that deals with keeping your mind free and healthy at a time when it is getting harder and harder to tell the difference between corporate entertainment and advertising. A typical issue of the zine will talk about the weirdest McDonald's ads and the history of "flash mobs." I caught up with the editor and publisher, Carrie McLaren, to find out how she thinks we can "stay free."

You run a zine called Stay Free. *What kinds of things do you talk about in it?*

We write about media and consumer culture. Generally, we focus on how things like advertising and television affect us in ways we don't usually think about.

What do you mean, "stay free"? Aren't we already free?

The name is a spoof on the popular brand of maxi-pads, but there are always things that can limit individual freedom: having to work a crappy job for little pay, for instance.

How did you get interested in marketing and consumerism and advertising?

My first memory of being disgusted over advertising is when I read about Girl Scouts selling advertising on their badges. I was a Scout.

What sort of relationship is there between pop culture and marketing?

These days, pop culture is marketing. Take television. If you ask most people what television is for, they'll say it's for entertainment. But television, like all of the traditional mass media outlets, is first and foremost a vehicle for delivering audiences to advertising. Which is to say: selling things is more important to television than entertaining. The same thing applies to movies, commercial radio, websites, and, increasingly, video games.

What kinds of things do we need to be aware of when we watch a movie or a TV show?

The main thing to keep in mind is that our media outlets are businesses, and their first goal is to turn a profit—not to inform or even entertain, though obviously they can be fun to watch. So if you're only watching mainstream commercial stuff, you're missing a lot. To be a reasonably well-informed, intelligent human being, you need to do a little work—to seek out noncommercial sources, from varying viewpoints.

What advice do you have for young people who want to respond to corporate pop culture by making their own shows, movies, zines, and music?

A sense of humor will take you a long way.

Find out more about Stay Free *and read Carrie's blog at www.stayfreemagazine.org.*

is always shifting and changing, so don't be shocked if your favorite independent band or record label suddenly reappears owned by a giant corporation. These things happen because the corporations can offer the chance to reach much larger audiences, which often translates into making a lot more money.

That brings me to the final big problem with independent pop culture: quality. In corporate culture, you have professionals who are hired to make something look and sound a certain way. In indie culture, things are sometimes done quickly and on the cheap, and often the results are an unpleasant surprise—even to the creators. So a lot of independent productions don't come out quite right for whatever reason. You end up having to sit through some pretty awful things—people recording songs in which they swear non-stop and pretend they are gangsters; websites that are nothing but pictures of someone's vacation with their dog; blogs that talk endlessly about the contestants on *Idol*; bad horror-spoof movies in which a guy dressed up like a gorilla chases people around a dark basement.

Independent pop culture can be all over the map, and when it's bad, it's usually really really *really* bad. This is different from mainstream corporate culture, which almost always maintains a certain flashy quality, no matter how bland and predictable the love song or movie is. So while corporate pop culture is often boring, it is at least consistent. Indie pop culture is different—you never know what to expect. At the same time, if you can get through some of the stuff that isn't so good, you can find the gems.

And In This Corner...
Indie vs. Corporate

When I talk about how great it is that more and more people are making their own pop culture, I sometimes get a strange reaction: people don't like the idea. They say, "But if everyone is making

9 788420 532318

Focus on the Product

COMPANIES USE FOCUS groups to find out what people think of the ending of a new movie, the pilot of a television sitcom, or the catchy chorus of a pop song. In these marketing exercises, a roomful of teens might be shown the latest teen drama featuring 28-year-olds acting like high school kids. The teenagers attending the focus group (who do so because they are promised free stuff) are then asked to say what they think about the plot, the characters, etc. If enough people don't like it, then it's back to the drawing board.

Even once something is released, it can be subject to focus groups. According to the *New York Times*, the giant company Clear Channel, owner of radio stations across America, uses a "call out" scheme to decide what to play on their stations. After a song has been played 150 to 200 times, listeners are phoned at random and played 10 seconds of the song. If enough people say they've heard the song before and like it, Clear Channel adds it to their playlist.

Some people say that focus groups end up encouraging companies to make their products bland and boring, since anything controversial or interesting is bound to offend at least somebody. Others defend using focus groups because that's the best way to make sure companies are telling stories that people actually want to hear. What do you think?

their own movies, how will I know what to watch? So much of it will be *bad*." In other words, when there are just a few options made by professionals, you can sit back, relax, and not worry. When there are thousands of channels to choose from, as is becoming the case with Internet TV, blogs, and zines, then it's up to you to decide what to watch, read, or listen to. And there's no one filtering out the truly bad stuff and providing quality control.

My answer to this is: don't be afraid. Communities and individuals will rise to the challenge. Just as there will be more to choose from, there will be more people who make it their business to tell us what they think is really great and worth checking out. We have to decide for ourselves, of course, but there will be plenty of people out there compiling Top 10 lists and weekly recommendations to help our decision along. Already there are people who do nothing but point us to the best indie websites, online radio stations, and blogs. Inevitably, compelling storytelling and those who are tapping into the spirit of the times will attract a big audience. When people tell us about their lives and experiences, those stories are often raw and truthful and fascinating—even if they don't star a perfectly airbrushed celebrity.

Further Reading

Bitch Magazine: A Feminist Response to Pop Culture

Hello, I'm Special: How Individuality Became the New Conformity by Hal Niedzviecki

★ *Made You Look: How Advertising Works and Why You Should Know* by Shari Graydon

No Logo: Taking Aim at the Brand Bullies by Naomi Klein

Nobrow: The Culture of Marketing, the Marketing of Culture by John Seabrook

Stay Free magazine and website

www.popmatters.com

Do It Yourself

LIFE: THE MOVIE Create an advertisement for a movie starring your best friend, your parents, your sister, or your hamster. You can do a movie poster, a movie trailer, a radio ad, or an ad to be placed in a magazine. Your non-existent movie might be a romantic comedy, a horror thriller starring the family cat, or an action flick starring your dad. How are stories marketed and sold to us? What techniques seem to work the best?

WILL YOU BE MY HERO? Take a survey of friends, family, and people in your community. Ask them what their biggest dream is, and why. How many want to be scientists, politicians, police officers, or teachers? How many want to be famous football players, singers, or models?

SHOP TALK Ask stores in your community (coffee shops, restaurants, bookstores, art galleries, etc.) if they are willing to stock indie magazines, music, movies, or anything else made locally. Will they put up a poster for a poetry reading or band? If they say no, ask them why not. Will they consider changing their mind?

Keyword Search

media literacy

indie (independent) pop culture

celebrity (celebrities)

celebrity product endorsement

fame

Your Global Neighborhood Needs You

Creating DIY Pop Culture

DIY Rules: Welcome to a New Pop Culture

DIY stands for Do It Yourself. It's the kind of slogan you might see at the hardware store—Do-It-Yourself Bathroom Remodeling!

Don't worry. For some people DIY means going to the hardware store and comparing tap fixtures, but for us, DIY means doing stuff like recording your own radio show, publishing your own book, or filming your own video. DIY pop culture is the most important part of the independent pop culture movement.

Remember how indie culture was shown as a straight line pointing in both directions? Well, DIY pop culture creators keep that line growing. In fact, DIY pop culture is more like the drawing in the background—a not-quite-straight line that points in all directions with all kinds of crazy dips and tributaries. It's culture that keeps growing and changing and surprising us because it's made by us and, hey, who knows what's going to happen next?

Independent culture is the alternative to corporate pop culture. As we've already learned, it can cost a lot of money to make a movie, put out a glossy magazine, or start a radio station. That's why the DIY philosophy is: you don't have to be independently wealthy to create your own pop culture. If we work together and help each other, we can figure out how to do things on the cheap, on our own. We can change the world one project and community at a time.

The concept of DIY pop culture is that we are all capable of being our own entertainers and culture creators. It's just like back in the days before pop culture, when everyone in the community was expected to tell a story or do a dance or beat a drum at the weekly gathering. DIY says not only can we make our own indie pop culture, but doing so should be integrated into our everyday lives.

Unlike remodeling the bathroom, making pop culture doesn't involve stripping wallpaper and ripping out the old toilet. DIY is way more fun than that. But like remodeling, or building a website, or making a mixed CD for a friend's birthday, it is more work to do it yourself. That's part of the DIY spirit. You put in the effort and take responsibility for what you've done. You don't let others tell you what to like, you don't wait around to be discovered, and as much as possible you do everything by yourself for yourself.

Sci-Fi Fanatics and Weirdo Comics: A Quick History of DIY Pop Culture

DIY pop culture includes everything from illegal pirate radio stations broadcasting from moving boats to hippie communes to the origins of parts

of the Internet. Like all great cultural and artistic movements, DIY pop culture has a fascinating history. As with pop culture in general, DIY pop culture's development follows the invention and widespread use of different technologies. The more gadgets there are that let us record, broadcast, and create in different media, the more we are able to embrace the DIY ethic.

All the early pop culture was do-it-yourself. Inventors who came up with the first cameras, then film cameras and projectors, then video cameras, were also the first to use what they invented to entertain people. They had to do it all themselves. Who else would do it? So they didn't just make the machines, they also made the content to play on the machines.

Fast-forward to the time of mass production and we see both the early developments of corporate pop culture and the rise of DIY. In the 1920s and 1930s, science fiction fans started to write their own newsletters about their favorite science fiction paperbacks. They would send these newsletters around to each other and eventually the newsletters became known as "fanzines"—magazines produced by fans. By the 1960s, a time of experimentation with all kinds of new ideas about society, the idea of putting out your own newsletter had spread. Now all kinds of people were publishing independent magazines for all sorts

of reasons. And DIY movements were suddenly emerging not just in publishing but in music, film, and other areas of pop culture.

There wasn't necessarily a DIY pop culture philosophy at the time. Much of what was then called underground culture dealt with issues such as racism, women's rights, and the Vietnam War. At the same time, new kinds of independent art, music, film, poetry, comics, and even journalism were being created. Free weekly neighborhood newspapers started publishing, and featured a new style of "gonzo" journalism in which the writer didn't pretend to be just a "fly on the wall" reporting but actually told the story from his or her perspective. These newspapers and zines were also publishing a new form of comic—adult comics dealing with boring jobs, sex, drugs, rock and roll, and politics.

New forms of DIY pop culture encouraged the different social experiments that were also cropping up at the time. For instance, in downtown Toronto's famous high-rise communal living residence Rochdale, there was an entire do-it-yourself education system called Rochdale College. There were music studios where you could record your own songs, a film studio from which you could borrow cameras, an adjoining publishing house, and a theater troupe. Similar communes were cropping up in Berkeley, California, New York's

A Shockmeister Settles Down:
Interview with Friendly Rich

FRIENDLY RICH IS a do-it-yourself pop culture pioneer who loves to try everything and anything. He's danced naked on a stage wearing only the smeared contents of a jar of Nutella, and he's led 500 kids in a parade of noise through a local park. Musician, impresario, educator, and freak, Friendly is just the guy to tell us what being DIY is all about.

You are in a band, have released your own CDS, created your own comic book, and started your own festival of the independent arts. You also teach kids how to make their own instruments and create noise. What makes you excited about DIY culture?

I enjoy composing odd cultural statements that get people thinking. I enjoy creating entities like the Brampton Indie Arts Festival or the Lollipop People and seeing it/hearing it/smelling it mature over the years. I love the idea of people getting involved in their communities as artists. If you think your town is boring, then DO SOMETHING about it. We are quick to complain, but I do not see many artists making a difference.

What's the best thing about DIY?

It is very handy to have a great hand in steering how my work gets produced. However, it comes with the process of learning about many different fields. For example, a do-it-yourselfer will have to fake

like he knows what he/she is talking about in so many circles where the navigation is blurry. I enjoy this challenge, as an actor or a snake-oil salesman might. Through this process, I have educated myself in many areas where my education in music did not prepare me at all.

How do you get attention for DIY when there is so much corporate pop culture out there?

The creative side of my brain has always appreciated the art of marketing. How to make something stick out in a sea of dull is not that difficult. I have always worked in a world where the stuff I produce is so strange that it naturally sticks out to most people. I enjoy existing in a world where we cannot truly separate the ad from the artwork. I like being creative enough to make this work succeed. Part of being an artist is being creative enough to find your work some loot. In a world where webcasting, podcasting, and file sharing seems intimidating, I have never been more inspired to explore what's out there for every artist. If *I* can market my stuff to the world, then there's hope for all artists who want to do it themselves . . .

Greenwich Village, and elsewhere. Though much of this innovation began as a way to explore alternative political ideas, the concept that anyone could and should be free to make movies or rock music was one of the real, great legacies of that era. Such experiments formed the backbone of what we now think of as DIY pop culture. And many of the ideas that were radical in the sixties—like comics with grown-up themes or arts cooperatives where people band together to help each other make culture—are now things many of us take for granted.

By the time the 1970s came around and punk rock was emerging from Britain, companies were learning that if they wanted to keep up with the times, they would have to incorporate the look and feel of youth movements and new social trends into their products. It didn't take long for green mohawks, safety pins, and ripped jean jackets to appear on fashion runways and in glossy advertisements. The sixties and seventies' DIY movement lost momentum as more and more companies borrowed its ideas, sapping the energy and passion of pop culture movements and turning them into products.

Then came the 1980s, when countries including the U.S.A., Britain, and Canada entered an intensely conservative era. Business prospered, particularly corporate pop culture. Madonna was a hit, Bon Jovi was a hit, Cindy Lauper was a hit, *Star Wars* was a hit, and the biggest hit of them all, Michael Jackson, captured the fake glitz of that decade.

A massive global corporate pop culture emerged and started to take over. Governments were allowing huge mergers that formed giant companies, and slowly but surely fewer and fewer voices decided what we would have access to on our televisions, radios, and movie screens.

Searching for a way to create a different kind of pop culture and voice other opinions than the dominant conservative ones, people started

The old-style computers
of the 1950s were only
accessible to experts.
Bring on the PC revolution!

looking at new
technologies. This was
a time when huge strides were being
made in bringing products such as the hand-
held video camera to the consumer. I remember
my dad bringing home our first VCR and our first
home computer. But I was too young to know that
I was witnessing the beginnings of a DIY pop culture renaissance.

Changing Times: Meet the PC

The personal computer changed not only life as
we know it but also the ability of everyday people
to make pop culture. In the early 1980s, our first
PC was a big lumbering IBM that by today's stan-
dards would be totally useless. But for me and my
brother the machine was a marvel. We took turns
typing in simple text-based games in the Basic
computer language and played them till we were
bleary-eyed.

When I talk to teens in high schools about pop
culture and I explain that in my childhood the

Internet as we know it didn't exist
and no one had PCs, I am greeted
with blank stares and confusion. They
seem to think I'm 90 years old. But you
know what? Personal computers like we
have today have only been around for 20
years or so.

As personal computers became affordable, things changed very quickly. All of a
sudden you could perform complex tasks in
your own home without knowing too much about
codes and programming. An early Internet developed—not the World Wide Web we have now, but
something more like text-only files that could be
sent through the phone lines to other people. Hey,
don't laugh—it was pretty cool at the time. People
began to trade ideas about how to get computers
to do things like record music, edit movies, and
publish magazines. The home computer revolution was under way.

More people started using personal computers,
and related technologies were developed to help
you do things at home you could previously only
do in expensive studios. Video cameras, photo-
copiers, image scanners, home radio transmitters,
and four-track recorders were all made, marketed,
and adapted to work with that most powerful tool
of all—the PC. By the 1980s there were enough
people self-publishing for there to be a magazine

Vegan recipe zine *Ripe* doesn't preach politics; it just gives you alternatives to a meat- and animal-product-based diet.

ripe

issue 4

cinnamon swirl biscuits
zucchini date muffins
three kinds of polenta
reduced balsamic vinaigrette
chipotle black bean soup
maple roasted roots
fettuccini *no*-fredo
gambar dal
lime coconut cake
carob chai cake
flax maple cookies
... and 28 more!

a vegetarian cookzine

that did nothing but review zines. That magazine was *Factsheet 5*, which started in 1982 as a photo-copied zine and within a decade grew into a 200-page magazine with thousands of reviews of DIY zines, books, recordings, and websites. Today almost all of us have computers in our homes or have access to computers at schools and libraries. There are easy-to-use programs for editing film and video, designing and printing your own zine, recording and editing music, and making your own website. Since you've been old enough to type, you and your friends have probably been making DIY culture—without even knowing it.

Hey Man, I'm Against the Man – DIY Goes Political

DIY pop culture does not necessarily have to be critical of or in opposition to mainstream ideas. But it often is. Even today, when everyone and their cousin's dog has a blog, many people still associate DIY with radical ideas and crazy agendas to overthrow society.

The truth is, I've seen tons of DIY culture that isn't political or radical. From bands that just want to make noise to zines and websites celebrating retro pop culture icons like the Bionic Woman and Mr. T, there's plenty of indie pop that's as fun to make as it is to appreciate.

That said, a lot of DIY pop culture does talk about stuff that is political in some way, and often seeks to challenge accepted notions of how our society works. Videos, songs, and zines comment on everything from starting your own organic herb garden in the backyard to opposing global trade agreements to boycotting Hollywood movies. Even though more and more people are making independent pop culture, DIY hasn't lost its edge.

But you don't have to be a radical to give your project a political edge. Perhaps the most important thing to realize about DIY is that the very *idea* of do-it-yourself culture is a challenge to those who control what gets seen on TV or sold at the mall CD shop. DIY isn't just about making your own stuff; it's also about showing other people that, yes, you can and should be part of your own society's conversation, discussing everything and anything you want to put out there.

Independent pop culture gives people an entirely new set of options. If we make our own

The Andy Brown Project

Andy Brown's zine explores individuality by profiling people who share the name Andy Brown from all around North America.

culture, we don't need *them*! Every time you draw your own comic or sing your own song, you're challenging an entire industry that has spent decades telling you to just sit back and let *them* sing the songs and draw the comics. Even silly do-it-yourself projects like the zine by the Montreal publisher Andy Brown, profiling all the people he could find in North America named Andy Brown, are in some little way opposing the "system."

Motivation: the Lie of Fame and Other Pitfalls

Getting started on a DIY project is probably the hardest part of becoming a DIY indie pop culture creator. (Second-hardest part: finishing—more on that later.) You need a plan, you need inspiration, you need someone to say to you, "Stop thinking and muttering to yourself, and start producing!"

A lot of times we get intimidated by what I like to call the Lie of Fame. The lie of fame is like a virus that spreads through contact with the media. It's the corporate pop culture promise that, yes, you too could, should, and one day will be absolutely and wonderfully famous.

In recent years there have been more and more celebrities of all kinds. On top of the famous actors, singers, and sports stars we've had for a long time, we now have famous chefs, business-people, dieters, third graders, doctors, therapists, even teachers. What is the connection between all these different kinds of specialists? Pop culture. Corporate pop culture is always in the business of creating celebrities. The more "normal" people they show who have suddenly become famous, the more we seem to believe we could be next. The next ultra-special, totally normal celebrity!

This is the Lie of Fame. It's a lie because corporate pop culture is top-down. It functions by having all of us at the bottom, a few people near the top, and an even smaller number right at the top. If most or even some of us could get to the top, the whole tower would collapse under its own weight. There would be too many bloated celebrities weighed down by their jewelry and limousines and champagne bottles, and not enough of us "normal people" at the bottom to hold up the tower.

Normal has become a bad word in our society. Everyone has to be an expert, a genius, a budding

CULTURE JAMMING

ONE DO-IT-YOURSELF POP culture phe-
nomenon that has got a lot of attention is
culture jamming. The notion of jamming
comes from "jamming the signal"—trying
to stop a particular broadcast from reach-
ing its audience by messing with it.

Culture jammers take their inspiration
from the idea of blocking radio and television signals. But jammers aren't about
shutting things down. Jammers are usually
people who have made DIY pop culture
and are frustrated at how hard it is to get
attention for their work. They want to make
people aware that there are other kinds of
pop culture they can enjoy and create for
themselves. So jammers will try to reach
people by subverting or altering the corporate media. The idea is to shock people
into realizing what else is out there.

An example of jamming might be renting a billboard or even unveiling a tempor-
ary billboard over one already advertising a
sitcom. As we drive along the highway on
our way home from work, we suddenly see
a totally different message on the billboard
than the one we're used to. Instead of an
airbrushed celebrity announcing that their
show is on every night at nine, we see a TV
screen covered with a skull and cross-
bones and the message: TURN OFF YOUR
TV BEFORE IT'S TOO LATE.

Jammers have infiltrated websites,
taken over TV broadcasts, and more. A
great culture jam occurred when a group
calling themselves Guerrilla Media
inserted a fake newspaper into newspaper
boxes. The paper looked and seemed like
the real thing, but it had a message about
the need for more freedom in the media.

When it works, jamming sure gets
people's attention! Of course, jamming
isn't something you do just for fun, it's
something you need to really think about.
Some of this activity borders on the illegal.
Personally, I don't advocate breaking the
law in the name of pop culture freedom.
But there are plenty of ways to culture jam
without breaking the law. Try making a
zine that looks like your school newspaper
or filming a parody of your local TV news
and putting it up online. All do-it-yourself
pop culture is culture jamming in a way,
because it can get people to do a double
take. And asking people to see things in
a new light is always going to provoke a
strong reaction.

Retro example of culture jamming in which an anonymous critic paints a mustache on the visage of a seventies pop star.

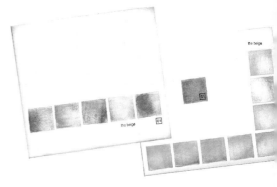

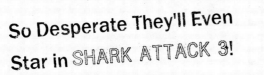

So Desperate They'll Even Star in SHARK ATTACK 3!

IN A *New York Times* article on B-movie actors, wannabe stars talk about entire careers spent searching for the big break. Despite years of barely making a living or working on the cheapest, lamest movies, these actors remain utterly convinced that fame is just around the corner. "I graduated fifth in my high school class," says Jenny McShane, whose work includes such straight-to-video classics as *Shark Attack 3*. "I was National Honor Society. I know I have the intelligence to do whatever job I have to . . . I want to do this till the very end. I want to be like Katharine Hepburn."

"I'll do whatever it takes . . ." says Tarri Markel, another 30-something actor, who so far has specialized in playing vermin and serial-killer bait in films like *Rats* and *Death Train*. "A break could come tomorrow or six months from now or six years from now . . . I don't have a time limit."

Are these actors victims of the Lie of Fame, deluded believers in the pop promise of fame for everyone? Or are they legitimate talents willing to do whatever is necessary to get discovered?

talent, an emerging star. But in truth we are all relatively normal, which is to say that, when you get down to it, we are all pretty much the same as one another, even those of us who are very talented.

The DIY pop culture philosophy is that it's normal to be talented, to have skills that other people don't have. That doesn't make you special and it doesn't make you famous. That just means you've latched on to the things that you're good at.

It's also normal to need a certain amount of attention. Everybody needs to be noticed and recognized by friends, parents, and other members of the community. However, corporate pop culture turns the normal desire for a certain amount of attention into an abnormal, all-encompassing drive for constant mega-attention. Corporate pop culture takes it as a given that what everyone wants more than anything is to be the center of attention all the time. That's why it focuses on selling the concept of celebrity—something we are told we should want that always seems just out of reach. But if we make pop culture because we think we're going to be celebrities, we're going to end up awfully disappointed.

Shock the Monkey: Can DIY Make Me "Edgy"?

These days everything is edgy, radical, crazy, and alternative. TV shows, bands, books, movies, and

the beige

with guest llynn kellman

saturday jan 28 9 pm

café montmartre 4362 main

When the band Beige released *01*, they took DIY seriously, hand-stamping each CD cover, then assembling each case manually. Their gig poster, too, extends the "handmade" theme.

all manner of products, from clothing to soft drinks, are supposed to be part of the "edgy" lifestyle. The problem is, if everything and everyone is edgy and underground, then what exactly is left for us to be alternative to?

This is one of the most difficult issues facing do-it-yourself pop culture creation. People often think they will show things in their movie that a mainstream corporation would never dare to show. But there is less and less that corporations won't put out there if they think there's a market for a certain kind of entertainment. Which means that people who make DIY pop culture because they think they are going to get attention by being as shocking as possible are doing it for the wrong reasons. Mainstream entertainment is perfectly happy to be as shocking and controversial as it needs to be to keep its monopoly on our attention. In fact, these days the mainstream stuff seems to go out of its way to cover territory that used to be discussed only in the "underground." So if you are trying to be edgy and radical, what are you really going to accomplish?

What is truly original in DIY pop culture is the idea that you might communicate stories and feelings for a reason other than making money. That

people should have the freedom to use pop culture media to speak to each other and their communities is the *really* radical and alternative idea behind do-it-yourself.

Getting Started (I'm Ready to Create ... So Now What?)

By now you're probably thinking—hey, okay, enough already! What are we waiting for? Let's get down to it!

And I say: Okay, what do you have in mind?

And you say: Uh, well, hmm...not sure yet. But something big. And cool. Really really kick-ass cool.

Cool. Okay. We'll get right on that...

Despite all the discussion, if this is your first time jumping into a DIY pop culture project, you're likely to feel a bit daunted. You're also likely to feel confused halfway into it when you're surrounded by equipment, papers, empty cans of Red Bull, and half your friends all standing around in your basement waiting to be told what to do. It's like standing next to Mount Everest and thinking, Oh, yeah, no problem, people climb the thing every day. But it's different when it's your turn, isn't it?

In the chapters ahead we'll be exploring different ways to get creative and interactive with independent pop culture. We'll look at everything

from self-publishing to pirate radio to home movies. Obviously, what kind of pop culture project you want to undertake is ultimately up to you. If you are visually oriented, you might be more drawn to comics, or animation, or videos. If you find yourself thinking in poetic rhymes, self-publishing your own poems in a zine could be the way to go. If you're always on the computer, then why not create your own website for fellow computer enthusiasts? If you're constantly humming a tune and drumming your fingers to the beat in your head, then I'm thinking you should be either recording your own album or making your own podcast or pirate radio show.

As you'll quickly discover, no matter what you do, you'll have to learn a lot and try new things. Independent pop culture projects rarely involve just one skill. Whatever you embark on, you'll end up dealing with a varied combination of computers, design/illustration, writing, sound recording, and even accounting! These days almost everything can be done cheaply and easily on the computer, so you should get accustomed to using that PC. If you can't draw a single stick figure, you'll want to stay away from art projects, but you'll still find yourself dealing with issues of design. Your zine, for example, is going to need a cover, and the overall project—whatever it is—will probably need illustration and certainly some layout. Websites and even video games have a written component, so brush up on your typing.

No matter what you pursue, there will be challenges. Don't be afraid to try new things, don't be afraid to screw up the first few times, and don't

The Pop Quiz on Plunder

PLUNDER EMERGED FROM the idea of borrowing familiar riffs and beats or using parts of a bunch of different songs to make an entirely new song. These days, plunder can be found in every art form. Writers will make up poems composed entirely of lines from advertising jingles. Films will be compiled featuring nothing but clips from other films. Plunder is essentially a technique to make works of indie culture. The idea here is that we can use shared pop culture images, phrases, snippets of songs, and jingles to create entirely new works.

A crucial moment in the evolution (revolution?) came in 1989. That was the year John Oswald, a musician, self-released the now-legendary *Plunderphonics* CD. The songs on *Plunderphonics* consisted of recognizable—though radically remixed—snippets from the songs of pop stars such as Michael Jackson and Dolly Parton. *Plunderphonics*, at the time, was a startling attack on pop music, a deliberate effort to reimagine mass culture as something we all have access to. The cover featured Michael himself, appearing as a naked woman from the neck down.

Anyway, to make a long story short: Jackson's CBS Records was aggrieved. They launched an action against Oswald and forced him to destroy the roughly 300 copies of the CD remaining. Today, however, the recording is alive and well, circulating on the Web.

Plunder is a big part of DIY culture, as it is often used both as an innovative way to tell a story and as a technique in culture jamming. These days, a great example of plunder is the trend to re-edit movie trailers for laughs. So the trailer for the horror movie *The Shining* is turned into an ad for a feel-good buddy flick. Plunder, you see, can be very funny.

Of course, as you have probably figured out, it is also a technique that can get you in plenty of trouble. Our shared cultural experiences mean that we immediately "get" plunder. At the same time, many creators and corporations object to plunder and try to protect their copyrights no matter how their work is being used or whether the process is completely not-for-profit.

So, the debate about plunder continues, and it's a fair bet that people will keep seeing what they can get away with. As a Columbus, Ohio, plunder musician by the name of Marc Gunderson once told me: "It excites me that there is actually music that is illegal. It's stunning and exciting and kind of motivational as well."

CELEBRITY WORSHIP SYNDROME

Celebrities, such as silent movie star Douglas Fairbanks (pictured here), revel in the worship while audiences are taught to be passive consumers of entertainment.

CELEBRITY, AND THE desire to have some kind of connection to the rich and famous, is getting out of control. So much so that psychologists at the University of Leicester in England have identified a mental disorder they are calling Celebrity Worship Syndrome.

Their study claims that one in three people in the U.K. suffer from the disease. Explains Dr. John Maltby, who reported on the study in the *Journal of Nervous and Mental Disease*: "Our findings suggest the possibility that many people do not engage in celebrity worship for mere entertainment. Rather, there appears to be a clear clinical component to attitudes and behaviors associated with celebrity worshipping."

In other words, it's not just fainting at the sight of your favorite band getting into their limo anymore. Celebrity worship is no longer a fun-loving, momentarily wacky thing people take part in when they are 14. Obsessive interest in celebrity has become an identifiable mental disease. The doctor and his colleagues have even classified three levels of celebrity worship. At its least troublesome, there are those who simply like to casually follow the careers and lives of certain celebrities. Those somewhat more afflicted believe they have "an intense personal-type relationship with their idol." Finally, there are what Maltby calls the "hardcore cws sufferers," who "believe their celebrity knows them and are prepared to lie or even die for their hero."

Remember the Lie of Fame? Well, think of Celebrity Worship Syndrome as what happens when people realize they aren't ever going to be famous but still desperately want the lifestyles of the glamorous and glorious. The cure for cws, like the truth behind the Lie of Fame, is the vaccine of do-it-yourself pop culture.

IDEA

A DOCUMENTARY ON A LOCAL MUSICIAN.

A REVIEW OF AN ARTSHOW

A CRITIQUE OF WORLD POLITICS

MEDIUM

WEBSITE

ZINE

DVD

be afraid to ask for help. When it comes to getting other people involved in your DIY pop project, you'll be surprised how generous everyone can be with their time and skills. And of course, if you can rope in a few friends and turn it into a group project, you'll have more ideas, more skills, and more collective energy than if you go it alone.

DIY Dos and Don'ts

★ DO plan ahead.

★ DON'T worry if your best-laid plans go somewhat awry.

★ DO take what you do seriously.

★ DON'T be so serious that you're not having fun!

★ DO try things you haven't tried before, ones that you think you aren't good at.

★ DON'T be afraid to admit that you aren't good at something and get help.

★ DO talk to your friends and family about what you are up to.

★ DON'T expect them to be as excited as you are.

★ DO expect that your finished project will be noticed and appreciated.

★ DON'T expect that you'll earn an Academy Award and enough money to buy a mansion on the beach.

Focus on the Idea

There are so many possible ways to create, and if you're like me, you want to do it all. But the truth is, the best projects come out of a single idea. In other words, you will achieve the best results if you focus on one idea and use one method of communication to get that idea out into the world.

Great, you're thinking, where do I get a cool idea for a pop culture project guaranteed to impress and amaze? Well, ideas are everywhere, and the best ideas come from what you know and have to deal with all the time. If you are thinking about something a lot, try writing some of those thoughts down in a notebook. After a few weeks, read over what you've written. If you notice four or five comments on the new ads plastered on the desks at school or on the local buses, then obviously this is a subject you're interested in. If, on the other hand, the experiences you have while getting your video game alter ego blown to bits are what you find yourself doodling about, then go with that.

Simple can be beautiful, as with this tiny zine of surprisingly evocative bird drawings.

That's what I mean when I say that ideas are everywhere. They are found in your everyday life experiences. Get curious about the world and your place in it, and you'll have more ideas than you know what to do with.

Deciding on a Project

Okay, so how are you going to turn your idea into a project? The goal is to match the method of communication—the medium you want to talk to us through—to the project. Which means now is the time to decide if you are going to make a movie, draw a comic, write a zine, put up a website, or record songs. If you are exploring, say, how advertising is filling up the public spaces of your community, then maybe you should consider shooting a short documentary video. Then again, a zine would be a good format for that kind of project too. You could include your personal rants—"Why I Hate That Billboard!"—and an interview with a local politician who is trying to restrict ads in your community, and maybe even a few spoof ads. For a project on first-person shooter games, a web-

site might be the way to go. You could put up tips, ideas for improvements and for new games, and a chat room where gamers can talk. Then again, maybe you want to do a radio show where you interview game makers and game enthusiasts. This could be a podcast, an MP3 file you email or burn for interested parties, or it could even be a show on a community or pirate radio station.

There are always pros and cons. Each medium comes with its own demands and limitations, as well as its advantages. You might find that you can't adequately capture the essence of video games through interviews, because you can't actually show the games themselves. So maybe a web project will be the way to go after all. Or you might find that a radio project is great, because you can concentrate on the ideas behind the games without getting that itchy-trigger-finger feeling of wanting in on the action. In the end, you need to experiment, take risks, and be prepared to get it not exactly right the first time out. Only by doing it will you learn what works best for you.

Finding Help

Help! I'm lost in a maze of wires, instruction manuals, scripts, photocopy machines, and Post-it notes. I don't know what I've got myself into and I'm really frustrated, so . . . whatever . . . I guess I'll just give up.

Hey—don't give up just yet. You still have that one great resource to call on: the rest of the world. The beauty of pop culture is that it breaks down barriers and creates connections out of shared interests. So when you're stuck, most of the time all you need to do is ask around for a helpful shove forward. Here are some ways to get help:

★ Ask your friends. You've never used script-writing software or drawn a comic before, but maybe they have.

★ Want a website where people can go to learn more about your anti-advertising campaign but don't know how to make one? Why not cross the lunchroom and make friends with the nerdy kids you're secretly afraid of because they can read your email just like that? Make new friends and alliances based on who's interesting and maybe even interested in what you want to do.

★ Of course, there's also plenty of help to be found in more traditional resources. Ask your school and public librarians if they have books on how to do what you want to do. Search the Web and find sites dedicated to home movie making, home audio recording, self-publishing, etc.

Write What You Know and Other Cheesy but Effective Ways to Think Up a Good Idea

★ THE OLD saying goes: Write what you know. The same is true for any creative act you want to embark on. Draw, sing, film, broadcast, and publish what you know, too!

★ DON'T BE A COPYCAT. Imitation is flattery and flattery is just sucking up. If, suddenly, your concept for a story about a group of travelers marooned on a weird island after a plane crash seems *done*, maybe you need to go back to the drawing board.

★ GREAT STORIES can't emerge out of "ho-hum" and "whatever." You have to *feel*. Are you angry about something? Ecstatically happy about something? Write down what you are feeling while you are in the moment, then try to figure out how you can use that powerful emotion as a way into an idea.

★ TAKE YOUR TIME. The concept for a project might not come to you right away. It might take weeks or months. The next-door neighbor's obsession with getting the greenest lawn ever might be your inspiration. Or that cool, mysterious stranger who suddenly sits down next to you in math class might have the key to unlock your ideas. Be patient. It'll come.

"Mistress of the Empty Girls"

Interview with Emily Pohl-Weary

EMILY POHL-WEARY EDITS and publishes a zine called *Kiss Machine*. She writes fiction and poetry, has developed the plot for a video game, edited a book called *Girls Who Bite Back: Witches, Mutants, Slayers and Freaks*, and is working on a series of books for teens about a girl detective. She's also in the midst of writing and publishing a four-part series of comics called *Violet Miranda: Girl Pirate*, about two girls who find adventure on the high seas. We caught up with her to find out more about her DIY career.

You've created zines, video games, and comics. How do you come up with ideas for projects?

If I'm inspired by something, like indie video art, role-playing games with female heroines, mystery novels, or superhero comics, I become temporarily obsessed and consume everything that's been created in that particular genre. I also can't stop my brain from coming up with new, similar projects that add to the public consciousness, the library of existence.

How do you manage to turn an idea into something you actually do?

Ideas and actions are inseparable for me. When I get an idea, I'm kind of like a pit bull and won't open my jaws until it becomes a reality. The name Emily actually means "the industrious one," and I feel like in some ways I've been living up to it my whole life.

What's the most fun you've ever had making indie pop culture?

In terms of pure pleasure, I'd say the small crafty tasks, like hand-painting all 400 covers of the first issue of *Kiss Machine* with my friend Paola Poletto, or decorating the display materials I use to show off my wares at zine fairs and conventions-— things like my star-festooned tablecloth and sparkly pink easels. There's a limited time frame and no pressure, so I can just enjoy the process. Plus, I really like to get my hands dirty.

What's been the biggest challenge you've had to face?

Worrying what my family will think of my weirder writing, and figuring out how to make a living.

You've done so much stuff, yet you're not even famous. Why aren't you disappointed?

No. 10 The Disposable Issue

KISS MACHINE

It's bizarre to me that you consider fame so important. It's overrated. I grew up in a family with two famous grandparents and realized that it didn't solve anything. In fact, it makes some things more difficult. Having goals you can actually achieve means that any disappointment is quickly overwhelmed by success.

For more info about Emily's work, visit http://emily.openflows.org.

★ Check in with the professionals. Ask your parents and their friends if they know anyone who, say, writes commercials or designs websites or works as a lighting technician. Bet you didn't know that your math teacher used to perform live as an Elvis Presley impersonator and your mom's best friend had a stint working on movie sets.

What to Say to People Who Tell You that Pop Culture is Just a Stupid Waste of Time

Some people will tell you that making your own movies or websites is a waste of time. After all, there's plenty of that stuff out there—who needs more? Parents, teachers, even friends might think you are far better off honing your skills as a concert pianist or rewriting your college application essay than doing a blog about your town or a documentary about the local dog pound and the plight of abused puppies. Or they may say that if you have so much free time, you should get a job and make some money. I hear they're hiring at the local Pizza Hut.

You can tell them that pop culture is just a way to communicate with each other, like giving a speech or writing a letter. Are those things a waste of time? And, yes, there's plenty of stuff out there, but it's not your stuff, it doesn't say what *you* need to say.

You can also tell them that you are learning more making your zine or podcast or movie than you would in a thousand years at Pizza Hut. Yes, you could use the extra pocket money, but these are the kinds of skills that are really valuable and can land you a plum job that doesn't involve asking about thin crusts and extra cheese.

Your friends might be disappointed in the finished project. They might think the acting in your movie is amateurish, or your comics could have been funnier, or your first album's songs don't rock hard enough. You can tell them that you're interested in their opinion—would they be willing to help make the next issue of the comic better?

A DIY Pop Culture Manifesto

You're about to embark on a journey that, hopefully, will last a lifetime. So let's end this section with some words that you should keep in mind no matter if your project has a budget of $5 or $5 million.

★ I have the right to express myself by producing pop culture myself, my way.

★ I have the right to enjoy and appreciate other works of DIY pop culture from my community and all over the world.

★ I have the right to not want to become a celebrity or anybody famous—I just want to do my thing.

★ I have the right to not want to make millions of dollars from my DIY pop culture—I just want to do my thing.

★ I have the right to tell stories about my life and my community, stuff I don't read about in the news or see on TV.

★ I have the right to learn from my mistakes. I screw up and then I do it all over again, because pop culture doesn't always have to mean slick and brilliant.

Further Reading

DIY: *The Rise of Lo-Fi Culture* by Amy Spencer

Everything Bad Is Good for You: How Today's Popular Culture Is Actually Making Us Smarter by Steven Johnson

Free Culture: How Big Media Uses Technology and the Law to Lock Down Culture and Control Creativity by Lawrence Lessig

★ *Hey Kidz: Buy This Book! A Radical Primer on Corporate and Governmental Propaganda and Artistic Activism for Short People* by Anne Elizabeth Moore

Inventions: Great Ideas and Where They Came From by Sarah Houghton

Jamming the Media: A Citizen's Guide to Reclaiming the Tools of Communication by Gareth Branwyn

Making Stuff and Doing Things: A Collection of DIY Guides to Doing Just About Everything! by Kyle Bravo

We Want Some Too: Underground Desire and the Reinvention of Mass Culture by Hal Niedzviecki

Do It Yourself

REPORTING LIVE FROM SOME KID'S BASEMENT, THIS IS... Do a short news segment on someone who is making DIY culture in your community. This could be a radio or TV news spot or an article for the entertainment section of your newspaper. How hard is it to find DIY pop culture creators? How is a news spot on a DIY creator different from one on a Hollywood movie star?

JAM THE CULTURE Find a magazine ad or a billboard you judge offensive, misleading, and/or just plain stupid. Make your own ad that tells the truth about the company or product and gets your friends laughing in the process.

POP STAR, KNOW THYSELF Ask someone you know only a bit to interview you. Get them to ask you about your favorite things to do, what you worry about, what you love, and what you hate. Tape the interview and then play it back to yourself. See what ideas emerge.

IN THE BEGINNING... Write/draw a comic telling the story of how your favorite book, TV show, song, movie, or piece of art came to be created. How did the creator get his or her first idea? What kind of work went into turning the idea into an actual thing others could experience?

I CAN TOUCH MY TONGUE TO MY NOSE Make a list of all the skills you have that might be useful in making a pop culture project. Can you draw? Act? Sing? Do makeup? Program flash animation? When you are done with your list, move on to your friends, your parents, their friends...By finding out what skills everybody has, you'll know whom to turn to for help—and you'll probably hear some surprising stories, too!

Keyword Search

DIY (do-it-yourself) culture

plunder/*Plunderphonics*

culture jam/jamming

creativity

motivation

celebrity worship/obsession

pop culture (learning from/is good for you/ and creativity)

great ideas/inventions

PART
TWO

FROM ACTING TO ZINES: The A–Zs of Making Your Own Pop Culture

4

Starting the Presses

Zines, Comics, Books

The Printing Press and You

Practically ever since the written word was invented, people have been using it to get out their feelings, ideas, and points of view. From the 16th century on, politicians, economists, poets, comic artists, journalists, activists, and philosophers have self-published everything from big statements on the rights of humanity to fad diets guaranteed to promote eternal life to guidebooks on the best way to use your car's engine for cooking your dinner. These days, with all those TV shows and movies and video games out there, printing your own self-published zines and even books might not seem like the coolest method of starting your DIY pop culture career. But rest assured, you are taking your place in a time-honored tradition of freethinkers, rabble-rousers, and dreamers.

There are all kinds of ways to self-publish. Zines—which are generally photocopied—are the easiest to start with. But you can also self-publish newspapers, comics, webzines, even books. It depends on what you want to achieve, and what your budget is, of course. One day you might graduate to starting your own full-color glossy magazine. Or you might want to publish a monthly community newspaper. You might even decide to collect all the comic strips you've published in your various zines over the years and publish them in a book.

All those things are possible, but they are hard work. So why self-publish? I've got one word for you: *freedom*. More than any other independent pop culture medium, self-publishing lets you create quickly, easily, and without a lot of complicated technology. If you want to, you can make a zine entirely from stuff you already have in your house. And to get started you don't need computers or any kind of electronic devices at all.

In short, putting out your own magazines, comics, pamphlets, or wild and crazy thoughts on everything from garden gnomes to girl–guy relations is relatively easy, a lot of fun, and a great way to show off how fascinating you are.

Warning: Writing Ahead

You might as well face up to it: that mini-magazine you are planning will require writing. Even if you want it to be mostly collages of cut-up images or just free-form drawings, an introduction addressed to your readers is a very good idea.

Anyway, there's no reason to be afraid. Writing isn't easy, but—like most things you have to work at to be good at—the more you do it, the less you'll feel like you're sinking in quicksand.

I Can't Write

Wrong. Nobody is expecting you to be the next Shakespeare. If you write the way you speak and think, you'll be fine. The worst thing you can do is try to write in rhyming couplets with lots of *thous* and *shalls*. Nobody talks like that anymore, and nobody wants to read what you have to say when you're trying to sound like somebody you're not. So just write naturally. Write the way you hear the words in your head.

Everybody can write. You don't have to be a literary genius. You're just trying to express yourself. And that doesn't take any special knowledge or expertise. Just don't expect that, the first time you sit down to write something for your zine, it will all pour out exactly how you want it. The first time you write, it may seem like a horrible chore. But if you keep at it, eventually you'll find that you have your own distinct voice that comes out pretty easily.

Of course, hearing what you want to say in your head and writing it down so that others can also enjoy your stories and ideas isn't the same thing. Be prepared to rewrite, edit, and revise. Remember that a story or a poem or just observations of everyday life will be better if you reread what you've written and delete all those typos and spelling mestakes.

What's a Zine?

A ZINE IS an easy format to self-publish in. It is basically a mini-magazine. Drop the "maga" from *magazine* and you've got *zine*. Zines are usually published cheaply in photocopied editions of a couple of hundred, and they are generally the personal project of one or two people. They aren't made for profit, but as a way to get ideas and stories out into the world. As I mentioned in the last chapter, zines developed in the 1930s as a way for science fiction fans to share their enthusiasm about sci-fi books. Originally, these mini-magazines were called fanzines, because they were self-produced by fans of sci-fi. But since then, zines have shrugged off the "fan" label and developed a reputation as a no-holds-barred format for publishing. These days, some people publish zines online in website or "webzine" format. Much of what is discussed here is applicable to webzines, blogs, ediaries, and other forms of online publishing (see chapter 7).

Writing Dos and Don'ts

★ DO write about everyday things: your friends, your school, your favorite foods, how annoying your little brother is. But also why they're cutting down the forest behind your house to make room for another road, or why most kids can easily identify 20 brand logos but can't name the majority of the plants growing in their local park.

★ DON'T try to write a huge multigenerational tale set in a 15-planet galaxy one million years from now. Keep it simple to start off with. Nothing wrong with using your imagination, but try to keep the project small, something you can finish. You can always turn it into a bigger project (such as a book) later on.

★ DO experiment with different kinds of writing. Try poetry, short stories, and diary entries to get what you want to say across. Sometimes a topic can be better explored if you approach it as if it were made up. Say there just happens to be this girl who just happens to be dealing with breaking up with her boyfriend and just happens to be feeling like she's going to have a nervous breakdown at any moment. You can see how throwing in fictional details might help you approach otherwise very personal stories. (Especially if you don't want to mortify anyone, including yourself, with what you print.)

★ DON'T be in a huge hurry. Writing can take a while. Plan to spend a few weeks just writing before you move to the editing and revising stage.

So What Should I Write About?

That's up to you. But a great rule of thumb is— write what you know. If you write from your personal perspective, you can be sure that you'll be telling us stuff we don't know. After all, how are we supposed to know what you're thinking about until you tell us? As well, writing what you know, at least to start, keeps it fresh and natural. If you want to pen long essays about saving the whales or how much you love the original *Star Wars* trilogy, that's okay. But keep in mind that lots of other people have written at length on these subjects, so you need to find a different angle if you're going to keep your reader interested. Again, the best angle is often personal: the first time you saw a whale when you were on vacation with your parents; how you used to love your light-saber when you were six years old. Stuff like that can make any topic interesting, no matter how many times it's been written about before.

"Write what you know" is good advice, you're thinking, but what if I don't know anything? After all, I'm still in school.

Well, you probably know more than you realize. If you're stuck for something to write about, start by describing your bedroom. You know it pretty well, I bet. Talk about what's on the floor, on the shelves, under the bed, in your iPod. See where that takes you. Pretty soon you'll be talking about all kinds of stuff you suddenly realize you know: what's happening in your school, in your family, in your neighborhood. Your favorite books, movies, music. What you regret you did to fit in, what you wish you had done to fit in, why you pretend you don't care about fitting in when you really do. But even if you want to write about a plucky young teen who suddenly finds out that she is the world's only hope in a coming battle against space aliens, that teen is going to be more interesting if she has problems we can relate to: parents who work too much, friends who talk behind other people's backs, maybe even the occasional skin blemish that no amount of acne cream seems to be able to get rid of.

Focusing on Your Theme

Okay, so you're over your fear and you're prepared to entertain the idea that writing about a seemingly boring existence can be more interesting to your readers than your thoughts on the life of a pop star, space aliens conquering earth, or how to lose weight in three easy steps. But how do all those unformed thoughts in your head become a great idea for a zine, or even a comic or an entire book?

Take a look at what you've been writing, doodling, and otherwise thinking about. Any themes or topics that keep coming up? Sometimes you'll surprise yourself. You think you're just rambling,

DONUT MUTATIONS

Zine Creator Profile:
CORNFLAKE REBELLION

Name and Age: *Betty Beehive, 17*
Hometown: *Perth, Ontario*
Zine: *Cornflake Rebellion*

What's your zine about? My zine is always shifting . . . it's what I need it to be at the time. Whether it's random rambling, stick figures, or photographs and poetry, it always reflects on who I am at the time.

How did you get into zines? I found out about zines through a friend and, without really knowing what they were, slapped together the odd mess that is *Cornflake Rebellion.*

Why zines? I love the glue sticks, the scissors, and the feeling I get when I've stayed up all night pouring every part of myself into a page of my zine.

What advice do you have for those starting out? Jump right in. Don't worry if you don't know exactly what it's supposed to end up as, you'll learn so much faster if you just do it.

What do you want your zine to accomplish? I hope to grow through my zine and share that with the people I know, and the people I don't.

How can people find out more about your work? lady_laughs_alot@hotmail.com or www.geocities.com/cornflakerebellion.

but you keep mentioning the same subjects over and over again. The great thing about a zine is that it can be about almost anything; you can even do a zine on several different subjects. At the same time, your readers will be most interested if your zine is focused. You don't just want to ramble on about anything that comes into your mind the way you might in your diary or even a blog.

So read over what you've been writing and thinking about. Anything stand out? Say you've been going to a lot of different donut shops lately. You and your best friend have been really into weird donut shops and their weird specialties. Just who thought up the Hawaiian donut, anyway? And what's up with the *cruller?* Suddenly you've got an idea for a zine—the donut zine. In which you talk about why you love donut shops, you review some of the more outlandish donuts you've encountered, you interview the elderly woman who's always at the donut place at the mall, and you research and write about the history of the Hawaiian donut.

Zines often work best when they take on a specific subject and look at it from different

angles. Write about you and your best friend on the hunt for the coolest donut shop in town and you might discover that what you're really writing about is you and your best friend: the fights you've had, the great moments you've shared together, your plans to go to the same college and be roommates and never argue again.

Sometimes stuff that seems just plain silly can turn out to be about pretty important things.

And sometimes stuff that seems really serious can be pretty funny. Say, for instance, your parents are divorced and you keep writing about that, how it sucks to only see your dad on weekends and how you keep hoping they'll get back together even though you don't think it's very likely. You could do a zine about divorce, writing about how you felt when you first heard the news, some of the things you did to cheer yourself up. A great approach might be to try to do a funny zine about what you are going through. You could make an obnoxious list of the best ways to get things out of your guilt-ridden divorced parents. Other kids going through the same thing might just appreciate, and get a laugh out of, your so-called advice.

Point is, your idea can be serious, funny, or something in between. And you don't have to have it all totally figured out before you decide what you're going to do. You just have to

FOUND IS A zine that consists entirely of notes, diaries, and photos found by strangers and mailed to the zine's creator, Michigan's Davy Rothbart. The idea is pretty simple: people find stuff on the street or in the garbage or in the hallway of their school and send it in. Using this weird idea, Rothbart has turned his DIY project into two books, appearances on David Letterman, and, more importantly, an ongoing fascinating look into everyday life. Notes from angry girlfriends, snapshots of kids eating ice cream at the zoo, letters written by hopeful job applicants—all this regular stuff ends up in *Found* instead of in the garbage. As we read the zine, we wonder who these people are, what they are doing now, and why they threw away that photo or letter.

Some samples include a letter that ends, "Why would I take your stuff, when I can get my own? . . . Love, Mom" and a communiqué from a jilted girlfriend that says, "Mario I hate you—You're a f***ing liar—ps page me later?" There are also grocery lists, to-do lists, and family beach vacation snapshots.

With *Found*, Rothbart shows us how what people throw away tells us as much about who they are as what they keep. It's a great example of a zine that uses a simple idea to make a very interesting statement about how our lives are different but all the same.

For more information about *Found*, visit www.foundmagazine.com.

recognize that this is something that means a lot to you—like donuts. Or parents!

If you're not motivated and interested, don't bother writing about it. You don't want to realize three weeks in that, in fact, you find donuts (and parents) totally boring after all.

Before you settle on a topic, sit down and challenge yourself to come up with a list of things that excite you about that topic and different ways you might approach it. You should be able to produce at least 10 different ideas for writing about your topic. Ideally, you should have so many ideas that your hand is cramping up writing them down and you can't wait to get started.

Then you know you're ready.

Scissors, Stapler, Glue: Making the (Old-School) Zine

Zines are the easiest, cheapest way to self-publish because they are easy to design and copy and make available to your friends and community. And speaking of friends and community, many zines are done by getting a whole bunch of different people to contribute, which takes some of the pressure off you.

So let's talk about how to make a zine. Keep in mind that much of this information (particularly how to actually produce a zine) also applies

to do-it-yourself comics, which don't have to be full-color, slick-looking, magazine-sized *Superman* things, but can be black-and-white and the size of a zine. There are tons of great indie comic artists out there who either started out using the zine format or still use it. So if you are planning on doing a comic, read on. (And for those who figure they are the next Dickens or Emily Dickinson, we'll have some brief thoughts on books later on.)

Like a magazine, the zine can contain all kinds of different things, including pictures, drawings, comics, poems, stories, articles, word games, and interviews. Somewhere pretty early in the process of doing a zine, you have to figure out exactly what you think should be in there. You already have your idea and you've done some

DONUT JUGGLING

writing. You know you're excited. So do you think your zine would be best if it was all poetry? Have your ideas pretty much been coming out as short stories? Or do you tend to write in little slice-of-life diary bits?

There's no rule in zine making. For your first effort you might want to try including several different styles of writing. Your zine can be full of all kinds of different stuff, so long as it remains thematically coherent. And what, you are probably wondering, does "thematically coherent" mean? It means there should be a central idea or theme that runs through the whole zine, no matter how you approach the subject. This not only keeps the reader interested, but also reveals different aspects of whatever overall topic you choose.

Take your list of ideas and see if any of them can be matched up to the following list of various forms that zine content can take:

diary	essay
poetry	short story
comic	collage
list	interview
advice column	letter to the editor
photograph	drawing
word game (crossword puzzle, word search, etc.)	

The more elements you can incorporate, the more lively and exciting your zine will be. This is particularly true in terms of mixing visual elements such as comics and photographs with written parts. So you might have a poem on half the page and a photograph on the other half. The photo could illustrate or relate to the poem, and the whole page would be related to the topic you've decided to focus on—donuts, divorce, or something else entirely.

Either way, it's a good idea to plan out your approach and include a good mix of visuals and writing. If you can't draw, don't worry. Ask a friend to draw the pictures for you. Or you can make a collage by cutting out pictures from magazines and mixing them together. Old photos make for great visual accompaniment too.

Now It's Really Time to Start Writing

By now you should have:

★ a theme—the big idea of the zine;

★ a list of the best ideas on what to put in your zine; and

★ some notion of how those ideas are going to be turned into different forms of content.

So, on your list of ideas might be: history of the Hawaiian sprinkle donut; interview with the scary lady who always sits in the corner

REGIONAL FAVES

HAWAIIAN nursing an extra-large coffee; my favorite donut shops ever. How are you going to write about these things? Hawaiian history is probably going to be an essay. And you will want a photo of a Hawaiian donut to go with it. The interview is, obviously, an interview. Better not ask her for a photo—she might think you're stalking her! So how about you try to draw her portrait to go along with the interview? Favorite donut shops ever: that could be a list, or it could be an essay, or it could be a diary of different donut shops you've been to and what happened at each one. How about a list plus a poem about your ultimate favorite? "Lights are dim/guy behind the counter scowls at me/I order a chocolate glazed." A few photos of your regular donut store haunts wouldn't hurt either.

Once your list of ideas becomes a list of writing and illustration projects, it's time to start writing. Sorry, can't help you much more than I already have with the writing. Writing is a lonely business. You're on your own for now.

Editing and Proofreading

So you've written. You've gone over the text what seems like 10 billion times. You've eliminated the part where you talk about how much you hate your brother or blurted out a friend's secret for everyone to read. (It's okay to tell the truth—but it's not okay to embarrass people or make them feel terrible.) Now all you have left is the great stuff you want to put out into the world. It's time to learn more about the steps involved in publishing.

Editing is when you read over what you've written and see if there are ways to make it better. Editing is always a good idea, because when you go over your writing, you usually find that you've used the same word over and over and over and over and over and over again. (See how annoying that can be for the reader?) How many times do we want to hear that the chocolate glazed at Donut Village is "awesome"?

Proofreading happens when you have finished your writing and editing and you go over the whole thing one more time, just looking for spelling mistakes, missing words, bad grammar, and other things you might not have noticed when you were concentrating on the ideas and stories.

Editing and proofreading are hard work, and it is a good idea to get a second set of eyes in on this process. If you are already working with a friend on the zine, then you can edit her writing and she'll edit yours. If you're working solo, try to find someone who might be able to read your work, suggest edits, and then proofread once it's all done. And don't forget to give him credit in the zine for all his help!

Zine Creator Profile: DUPPY

NAME AND AGE: *Ansis Purins, 28*
HOMETOWN: *Allston, Massachusetts*
ZINE: *Duppy*

What's your zine about?

Duppy is a collection of my comic strips. The stories feature my characters Zombre, a friendly zombie that lives in a remote forest, and Fux, a robot from outer space. Also, I do some reggae-music-related comics. A duppy is a West Indian ghost. I thought the title was appropriate for a new series that adheres to no particular story or character.

How and why did you get started publishing?

Complete control. And because nobody has offered to publish my work for me. I find doing the process effectively to be very difficult. I'm just starting to understand the basics of self-publishing.

What's your favorite thing about doing a zine?

I love to draw and create worlds. Thus comics was always the perfect choice for me as a creative outlet.

How do you get ideas for your zine?

Music, video games, movies, books. Especially weird stuff off the beaten path. I try to find things I'm interested in and then try to convey that interest to my readers in a (hopefully) entertaining manner.

What advice do you have for people making a zine or comic for the first time?

Make a things-to-do checklist. Also, make a list of all the things you could do better next time. When mailing your work to people, seek advice and criticism. I usually ask people to tell me what they thought of the books. The key to an artist's growth is accurate criticism.

What do you hope to accomplish or achieve making your zine?

I hope to expand what I can publish, meaning the sizes, stocks, and formats of comics in printed format. I'm exploring the option of a giant-sized silk-screened comic book. I'm also thinking of laminated comics stored in sacks of glow-in-the-dark membrane-like goo. Y'know, the normal stuff.

How can people find out more about your work?

Check out my site, man: http://ansis.tv.

A collage from the zine *28 Pages Lovingly Bound with Twine*.

Some ideas for graphics are:

DRAWINGS Simple black-and-white drawings to illustrate stories and poems.

COMICS If your friend spends all his time doodling comic strips during math class, why not ask him to make something for the zine?

COLLAGES Pictures cut out of magazines and mixed up. For instance, you might cut an image out of a hunting magazine, an SUV out of a car-and-truck magazine, and a soldier at war out of a newsmagazine to accompany your thoughts on how society seems to be getting more violent.

PHOTOS To illustrate your stories. (If you interview someone, take their picture; if you review a donut shop, snap a shot of the baked goods display…) Make sure your pictures are in focus and clear, with lots of good contrast so they will reproduce clearly (black-and-white is good, lots of gray is bad).

Graphics

The graphics part of the zine is the non-writing stuff. Graphics are important because they make your zine look good, break up big sections of text, and keep people interested and excited. You want to make sure you have lots of graphics in your zine. You can get your friends involved by asking them to draw and take pictures.

Layout

Getting your words into a format that can be reproduced quickly and easily is called *layout*. Basically, you have to position the text and pictures on the page so that they can be photocopied. This isn't as hard as it sounds. Because the standard zine is the size of a piece of regular-sized paper folded in

1 1 SHEET OF PAPER = 4 PAGES

4 SHEETS = 16 PAGES

2 FOLD YOUR STACK OF SHEETS IN HALF.

3 NUMBER EACH PAGE IN CASE YOU NEED TO SEPARATE THEM

4 START LAYING OUT YOUR ZINE.

← the DUMMY →

half, the number of pages in your zine will always end up being a multiple of four. Twelve pages is pretty standard, or 16, or 20, depending on how much content you have. So get a stack of regular 8½" by 11" paper—the kind you put into a printer or photocopier—and follow the step-by-step diagram above for making a dummy zine.

A *dummy* is the model that you experiment on (like the crash test dummies they use when testing a car's safety). You'll want to make a dummy in order to see how everything looks on the page and fits together. Since you're just experimenting at this stage, you can easily change things around if a poem doesn't look good next to an article or a picture is too big or too blurry.

Once you have written out or printed out all your text, and you have the material you need to illustrate your zine—comics your friend drew, collage images cut out of magazines, etc.—then it is time to lay out the zine. This is when you

assemble your text and images on the pages. Try fitting different parts of the zine on different pages and see how it looks. When you're happy with it, use a glue stick to fix everything in place.

You now have the one and only *master copy* of your zine. The master is basically the perfect, one-of-a-kind original zine from which you will make all the millions of copies you will send out into the world.

If you want your zine to look cleaner, you can lay it out on a computer. This involves getting your hands on some desktop publishing software, programs like QuarkXPress or PageMaker. Layout software can be expensive, but ask around and see if you can use someone else's. You don't need all the fancy bells and whistles, just the basics.

With a layout program, you would import your text from your word processing program and guide how it is laid out on the pages. Then you would scan in your pictures and other images and import those onto your pages. It's a bit of effort learning how the programs work, but in the end you have more options for fancier design and you'll achieve a much cleaner look. And since most photos are being taken by

Zine Profile:
INFILTRATION by Jeff Chapman

JEFF CHAPMAN WAS a nerdy suburbanite who just happened to publish one of the most influential zines of the last 10 years, *Infiltration*, the zine about "going places you're not supposed to go."

Chapman started *Infiltration* in 1996, when he was 23 years old, inspired by a lengthy stay in a hospital that led him to explore the weird off-limits nooks and crannies of the huge institution.

"To fight off the boredom," he once told me in an interview, "I took to exploring the building's darkened hallways in my bathrobe at night. I had a lot of morphine in me at the time, so traveling down to the morgue and up onto the roof seemed like reasonable things to do. The sense of danger and the rush of adrenaline those explorations provided was such a welcome antidote to the boredom of lying in my bed all day that it seemed to be just about the most fun I'd ever had. After that, I was hooked . . . on infiltrating, not morphine."

Readers of *Infiltration* also developed the addiction. The appeal of the zine was not just the excitement of surreptitious, even covert, tourism. It was also the way Chapman documented his exploits with precise, methodical notations of where he'd been and how you could get there too.

Despite the potential for being caught trespassing, Chapman's pioneering philosophy of urban exploration included a credo to tread lightly. Chapman pledged never to vandalize, steal, or invade the privacy of others. He preached a kind of eco-trespassing, carrying out what you bring in, and never sullying the virgin wilderness of sewers and forgotten tunnels.

"Breaking into a house or a shop is not my kind of trespassing," Chapman told me. "But I don't think it's even debatable that too much urban space is cordoned off as private. Virtually every spot in the city is private property, aside from the occasional grudgingly conceded parkette. Malls have replaced public squares. I don't really have a problem with this, as I'll take a building over a park any day; I just hope no one seriously expects me to suppress my natural human urge to explore my environment. I see big things for the hobby of urban exploration as the world fills up with more urban space, more abandoned buildings, more tunnels all eagerly waiting to be discovered and explored."

Jeff Chapman died at age 31 after battling liver disease. But his influential zine is credited with pioneering the urban exploration subculture that thrives today. So look twice at that geeky little guy sitting primly in your hotel lobby. He might be one of the people Chapman inspired, on his way to one of Chapman's dream infiltrations: "the tunnels under Moscow, the drains under Melbourne, or the luxury hotels of Las Vegas."

Chapman's website www.infiltration.org lives on, and just before he died he self-published his book Access All Areas: A User's Guide to the Art of Urban Exploration.

digital cameras these days, you might already have a lot of images stored as files. It's up to you if you want to do it by hand or by computer. You'll just have to decide if you want the world to think of you as the does-it-all-by-hand artsy type or as the tech wizard whose work is powered by the magic of the mouse.

Printing and Binding

Now that you've glued all the articles and illustrations into the master (or created a file and printed it out), you have your one-of-a-kind original you can use to make 10 or 100 or 1,000 copies. The cheapest way to make a lot of copies is photocopying. First decide how many copies of your zine you want to make. Don't overestimate. There's nothing more depressing than having 1,000 copies of a zine about donuts sitting in your closet waiting for you to come home from college. Start with 50 or 100 maximum. You can always reprint.

Use your master to make double-sided photocopies of the pages. Start with your first whole page; unfolded, it will have your front and back covers (on one side) and your first and last pages (on the other side). Keep copying until you are out of master pages! Then collate your zine by putting the pages of each copy into the correct order, folding, and stapling. Hold on—before you staple, double-check to make sure that, yes, the pages are in order. Now all you have to do is staple the pages in the middle along the spine. Presto! You've got a zine!

A few things to remember:

★ Photocopying is cheap, but it does cost money. Ask around—someone might have a photocopier you can use for free. Your parents may have access and a nice boss at work. Your school or library could be a possibility. Perhaps you have a friend who works at a copy shop who can give you a discount. Where there's a will, there's a way!

★ Color photocopying is pretty expensive, so unless you *really* need to show that Hawaiian donut in full color, you'll want to stick with black-and-white. You can still use color images in the collages you make from magazines, but keep in mind that, when you copy them, they will come out black-and-white and usually a bit darker than expected. You might have to play with the tone on your copies to get it right.

★ The hardest thing to find is an extra-long stapler. You need this to reach the spine of your zine so you can staple it together without

Can't draw? Use your imagination. Indie writer Judy MacInnes Jr. put her poems between cereal box covers. *Super Socco*, a chapbook of prose poems, later became part of *Snatch*, published by Anvil Press. (Chapbooks are just short books, 48 pages or less.)

bending it. Sometimes local copy shops will have them, and can lend one to you to do your binding in their store. But otherwise, a visit to your local office supply center will be necessary, and your extra-long stapler could set you back $40. Use it well!

When you are finished copying your zine, carefully put the master pages into an envelope or box and store them somewhere safe. When your zine becomes a big hit and you are getting mail from all over the world and everyone wants a copy, you will need to reprint, so don't lose those original pages.

When a Zine Isn't Enough: Printing Your Own Book

Did I hear you say you want to make a book? Well, if you've got 80 or more pages of stuff that only works if it appears all together in one package, then you're probably ready. But can you really make your own *book*? Of course you can. To produce a book, you would apply the same rules you did when you made a zine. You need content—lots of it!—that hangs together and doesn't seem random. And you need editing and proofreading. Then you would use a computer layout program (like QuarkXPress or PageMaker) to typeset the pages (get them ready for printing). It's actually pretty easy once you've decided on a page size and a general look for the text.

Once you have your book as a giant file in Quark or some other layout program, you have to decide how to get the physical copies made. Here comes the expensive part. Unlike a zine, you aren't going to be able to scam free copying and do the stapling yourself. Books need to be bound, because they are so thick. So there are really two possibilities. Bigger, more professional copy businesses offer a binding service. They'll do, say, 50 copies of your book with photocopied pages and binding. You can even throw in a color-copied cover. This won't look exactly like the books you see in

NAME AND AGE: *Iza Bourret, 28*
HOMETOWN: *Quebec City, Quebec*
ZINE: *The Happy Loner (and other titles)*

So what are you working on?

The Happy Loner is my current perzine [a zine that deals with personal stuff like relationships, family, whatever is happening in the creator's life].

What's it about?

The Happy Loner is a perzine about a girl who likes being alone and doing lots of things on her own but who is also interested in people and the world around her. A non-depressed, happy, friendly loner who does have her problems dealing with people but tries to come to terms with them and understand and figure out how to function and keep the balance between human contact, bonds, and boundaries. Public transit, people watching, reflections, weird hobbies, walking in the streets at night, personal ethics, DIY, individuality versus community/ the world, the environment, doing things your way . . . those are just a few themes you'll find in it.

How and why did you get started publishing?

I published my first zine in 1998. At the time, I was a big fan [literally, a groupie] of the Canadian band Moist. I followed them across Canada on tour and I met some girls in Edmonton who did a Moist fanzine called *Succumbing to a Higher Power.* I always loved writing and I had made photocopied comics when I was a kid, so I thought I had to make one! My Moist fanzine soon included personal opinions and became a perzine pretty fast.

What's your favorite thing about doing a zine?

Trading, getting mail, getting feedback, and seeing that I am improving my writing and designing skills.

How do you get ideas for your zine?

That's a tough question. Ideas can come from anywhere: a situation I'm living in, overhearing a conversation on the bus, graffiti I see on the street, or just a train of thought that started nowhere and ended up as a rant.

What advice do you have for people making a zine or comic for the first time?

Take some time to sit back and think. Take your time. Look at the final product before copying. If you are unsure of something, take it out or redo it. Be yourself. If you have ideas, take notes so you don't forget. Carry a notebook with you. Work on your zine when you're in a good mood, put some good music on, have some tea, work in a place where you won't be disturbed. Verify the page order before making copies. Verify the page order before stapling. Use ink not pencil. Don't be afraid to talk about your zine or distribute/leave it in unusual places. Take chances. Have fun!

How can people find out more about your work?

On my website: www.geocities.com/girl_w_cat.

Zine Profile:
THE HAPPY LONER

Self-Publishers through the Ages, Great and Otherwise

Thomas Paine, one of the early rabble-rousing self-publishers, helped bring about the American Revolution with his pamphlets.

Old-school protester: Martin Luther's independent writings on the Church led to a break within the Roman Catholic church and the establishment of Protestantism.

SELF-PUBLISHERS have changed the world. In fact, some of the most influential writing of all time was self-published. In other cases, self-publishers have been . . . well, let's just say they've managed to get themselves noticed! Here are profiles of some of the more interesting self-publishers through the ages.

THOMAS PAINE An English-born American pamphleteer and dreamer, Paine's 1776 self-published pamphlets *Common Sense* and *The Crisis* were so popular, they reached a greater percentage of the U.S. population at the time than does today's broadcast of the Super Bowl. Paine's pamphlets demanded American independence from England and helped bring about the American Revolution.

MARGARET ATWOOD Canadian author Margaret Atwood self-published her first volume of poetry, *Double Persephone*, in 1961, the year she graduated from college. The print run was only 200 copies. Since then Atwood has won many major literary awards, and she is considered one of the world's best writers.

ARTHUR AGATSTON In 1998 this guy began self-publishing several hundred copies of a pamphlet outlining diet ideas for his patients. A few years later, this pamphlet became *The South Beach Diet*, which kicked off the low-carb craze and changed the eating habits of millions.

AMANDA BROWN Self-published her first novel, *Legally Blonde*, as a print-on-demand book. It was eventually made into a movie starring Reese Witherspoon.

MARTIN LUTHER A German monk and scholar, in 1517 Martin Luther sent copies of his tract "95 Theses" to influential figures. The document was a protest against the corruption and abuses in the Catholic Church of the time. Eventually, after Luther was kicked out of the Church, the 95 theses would lead to the Protestant Reformation and the establishment of a major new branch of Christianity.

LAWRENCE FERLINGHETTI In 1953, this poet founded City Lights Bookstore in San Francisco. Soon thereafter, he self-published *Pictures of the Gone World*, his classic collection of poems, as the first of many titles to be published by City Lights Books. About 30 years later, he became the first living writer to have a San Francisco street named after him.

Ben Franklin
self-published
his own almanac,
invented stuff,
and helped out
with the writing
of the American
Declaration of
Independence.

BEN FRANKLIN Using the pen name
Richard Saunders, he self-published his
Poor Richard's Almanack in 1732 and
continued to produce the almanac for
another 26 years. Many of his famous say-
ings come from this magazine. Because of
the success of his printing and publishing
business, Franklin was able to retire at the
age of 42. He became one of the world's
greatest inventors and scientists (inventing
bifocals, the Franklin stove, and the lightning rod). He ended his life as a statesman
and one of the key founders of the United
States of America as a signatory to the
Declaration of Independence.

TODD MCFARLANE Formed Image Comics
with six fellow artists and proceeded to
self-publish the *Spawn* comic book in 1992.
The first issue sold 1.7 million copies.

bookstores, but it will be relatively easy to deal with and a good solution if you want to produce a thicker, self-published project in small quantities. And there are lots of different binding options, everything from a plastic coil to tape that looks more book-like. Overall, for quantities under 100 copies, this is usually the cheapest option; you should expect to pay around $4 or $5 a copy.

Another option is to investigate print-on-demand service, which involves working with a company that prints each book as it is ordered. The way this works is that there's an online description of the book, and when somebody orders it, the printer makes a copy from the file you've already given them. This is good because you don't have to invest a ton of money, but bad because you don't have a product to sell at your book launch.

If you want, say, more than 200 copies, you are probably better off going to an actual printer. Find some in the yellow pages and call them up. A book printer will take your file and print an actual paperback book. This will cost you. Figure on paying between $6 and $10 a copy. If you are going this route, you'll probably need to sell your book for about $15 a copy if you hope to get your money back.

So, it's fair to say that publishing a book is an expensive undertaking only to be done by those with a serious desire to 1) go into debt and 2) be the next J.K. Rowling.

Tim Conley assembled his short stories into the book *Whatever Happens*, published by the independent Insomniac Press.

1) Give it away or sell it directly to your friends, neighbors, or others in the community. With this method, you simply go up to people and ask them if they would like to read a copy of your zine. You might tell them that it's about your favorite donut shops and the history of the cruller. Ideally, your zine would be free, since the purpose is to get your thoughts out into your community, but it is also okay if you charge a little bit (to help make back your costs). Zines usually sell for $2 to $5, depend-

I'm not saying don't do it, I'm just saying to all you budding Virginia Woolfs out there: what's the hurry? Before you saddle yourself with high costs and the problem of having to store 300 books in your bedroom, try publishing your writing in zines and journals, and build up an audience so you know for sure that someone's actually going to want your tome.

Getting Your Masterpiece Read

Now that you've published, it's time for the world to see your genius! That means getting your zine into the hands of readers. There are essentially four ways to get your zine out there.

Giant zine fair Canzine, held every year, is an event where zine creators can sell their wares and meet like-minded creators.

ing on how big and fancy they are. Remember, the more you charge, the harder it will be to convince potential readers to check it out.

2) Sell or give away your zine in stores. Yes, there are a small number of stores that sell zines. If you have a local independent record store or bookstore or magazine store, they might just be willing to stock your zine. If you aren't charging, you just need permission to leave the zine somewhere in the store where people are likely to pick it up. If you are planning on charging, then you need to work out with the store how much of a cut they will take of the cover price. A store might ask for 25 percent of everything they sell, which is reasonable—after all, they have to pay their rent and their employees.

3) Sell or give away your zine through the mail. There are websites and magazines that list and review zines. In some cases, this is a matter of posting an announcement that you have a new zine about donuts and it is available from this address. In other cases, you might send the zine in to a publication in the hope that it will be reviewed or listed. In all cases, you want to include your mailing address or email address—some way for people who want your zine to contact you. If you are giving your zine away, mention that it is available for free for either the cost of postage or, ideally, a trade with some other zinester out there.

You never know what you'll get! If you are charging, you'll have to indicate that the cost is, say, $2 plus postage. A reasonable postage charge would be $2.

4) Have a launch party! This is a great way to gather potential readers together and have fun too. Make up some flyers, send out some emails, and invite everyone to join you in your basement or at the local coffee shop or in some other cool space where you can launch your zine. This will get you more attention than if you just start handing it out. You might have a band play at your event, or have readings from your zine, or show a

short video. Of course, if you're doing a donut zine, you'll want to serve donuts! Naturally, everyone who attends gets a copy of the zine either free or as part of the price of admission. Go crazy with the decorations and the entertainment. The more of a spectacle you make, the more people will be interested in your creation.

At the end of the day, it will be your great content that gets your zine noticed. If you write what you know and feel, and only put stuff in your zine that matters to you, then people will want to read it. So what are you waiting for? Start scribbling!

Further Reading

The Book of Zines: Readings from the Fringe
by Chip Rowe

*Broken Pencil: the magazine of zine culture
and the independent arts*

★ *Cartooning the Head and Figure* by Jack Hamm

The Factsheet Five Zine Reader by R. Seth Friedman

★ *A Girl's Guide to Taking Over the World:
Writings from the Girl Zine Revolution*
by Tristan Taormino and Karen Green

★ *How Writers Work* by Ralph Fletcher

Make a Zine! by Bill Brent

*Notes from the Underground: Zines and the Politics of
Alternative Culture* by Stephen Duncombe

Stolen Sharpie Revolution: A DIY *and Zine Resource*
by Alex Wrekk

★ *Whatcha Mean, What's a Zine? The Art of Making
Zines and Mini-comics*
by Mark Todd and Esther Pearl Watson

★ *Write Away! A Friendly Guide for Teenage Writers*
by Peter Stillman

★ *Writing Smarts: A Girl's Guide to Journaling, Poetry,
Storytelling and School Papers* by Kerry Madden

★ *The Young Journalist's Book: How to Write and Produce Your Own Newspaper* by Donna Guthrie

The Zine Yearbook (annual collection of zine
excerpts published by *Clamour Magazine*)

www.spannet.org—independent publisher
resources from the Small Publishers Association
of North America

Do It Yourself

**BROTHER'S ROOM SMELLS LIKE SWAMP! READ
ALL ABOUT IT!** Publish a household newspaper for
a day or two. If you want, make it a sensational
tabloid: *Grandma is a Space Alien!* Or else do it for
real. Front page story: an exposé on the road the
city is building behind your backyard. In the Business section: Dad gets a promotion. Under Arts:
a profile of your band. Sports: your sister's soccer
game.

PESTER THE PROFESSIONALS Track down a journalist, poet, scriptwriter, or any other kind of
scribe. Ask them how and why they do what they
do. Pick up some tricks of the trade.

WHAT'S WRONG WITH THIS STORY? Read all the
available local newspapers in your area. Ask yourself: Are they representing you and your community as you see it? Why not? What's missing?
What do they do that you couldn't? What could
you do that they don't?

A PICTURE'S WORTH A THOUSAND WORDS Make
an eight-page zine using only pictures cut out of
magazines, newspapers, and anything else you
can find. How does a collage tell a story?

Keyword Search

zines

independent publishing

self-publishing

small press publishing

desktop publishing

cartooning/drawing

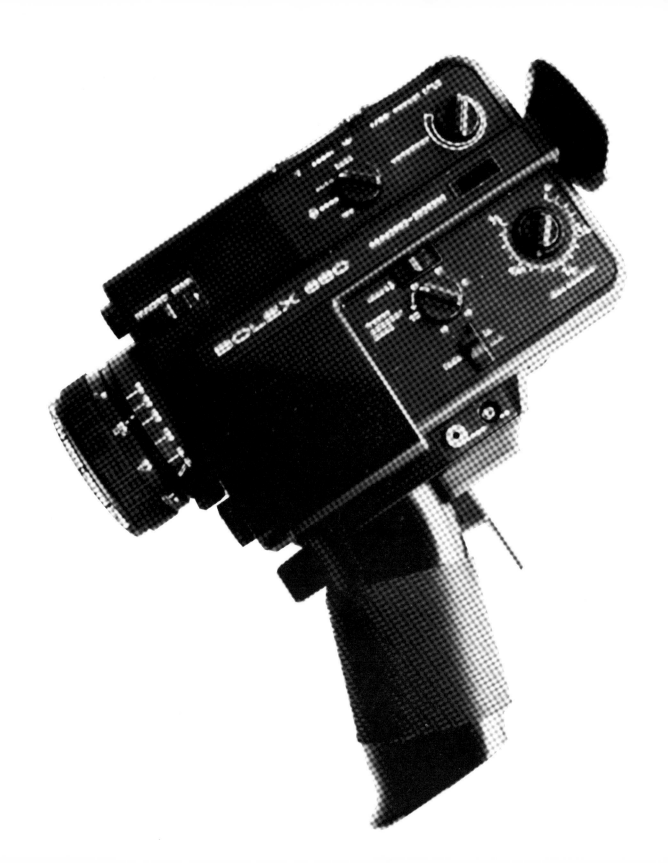

Moving the Picture

Making Your Own Cheap, Wonderful, and Probably Pretty Weird Movies, Shows, and Videos

Take a Picture, It'll Last Longer: Moving Pictures Make History

Lights, cameras, ACTION!

For those of us who grew up bathed in the glow of the TV, making motion pictures is less like a complicated task and more like a different way of speaking. We already speak film-talk, and can't help ourselves from seeing the world in close-ups and slow-mo moments. You know more about making motion pictures than you realize.

Because motion pictures are so accessible (there's that word again) they are virtually everywhere. These days, we watch TV and movies on cell phones and laptops, in planes, trains, cars, schools, waiting rooms, bathrooms, bedrooms, kitchens...Where *don't* we watch this stuff? By the time you're in your teens, you've already observed thousands of hours' worth. Studies show that the average North American kid watches 20 to 30 hours of TV a week!

We're so familiar with the conventions of television shows and movies, we often feel as if we know exactly what is going to happen next. Ever have the feeling right from the opening credits that you already know what will happen, how it will happen, and whom it will happen to? Makes you wonder if you couldn't think up a better story yourself between gym and math class. How many times have you turned to a friend and said, "Even *I* could do better than that"?

Of course, recognizing the predictability of TV shows, movies, and music videos is hardly

the same as actually making your own. In fact, you need quite a bit of practice and technical know-how to achieve something that doesn't look like discarded footage from *The Blair Witch Project* or home recordings of your little brother's bar mitzvah. Making short movies is probably the hardest thing to do on your own of all the pop culture creative endeavors. When you make a movie, you have to be ready to do everything from lights and cameras, to background music and dialogue, to directing actors and deciding on set design.

Becoming Your Own Personal Auteur

The world is awash with potential moving pictures just waiting to be ordered into ideas and stories and characters and emotions. And it seems so simple: just grab hold of Dad's video camera and get going!

But, as with all aspects of indie creativity, planning and thinking ahead will not only help narrow down the possibilities but will also help you tell the story you want to tell, not the one you see on TV 20 times a day.

So in this section we will look at three things to consider before you start pointing the camera at everything and anything.

Mule Skinner Blues:
Down and Out but Still Indie

IN THE INDIE documentary *Mule Skinner Blues* (2001) we meet the various inhabitants of a Mayport, Florida, trailer park. There's Beanie Andrew, a 66-year-old whose dream has always been to make a horror film in which he emerges from the primordial Southern swamp in a gorilla suit. There's rock 'n' roller Steve Walker, whose band plays local bars. There's the 70-something country yodeler Miss Jeannie, and the middle-aged janitor Larry Parrot, who methodically composes unpublished horror stories on an ancient manual typewriter. Is Mayport, perhaps, a hotbed of hopeful entertainers? Hardly. It's a hick town that the filmmakers stumbled upon pretty much by accident. Not unlike the better-known *American Movie*—in which filmmakers document the efforts of an impoverished film buff trying to shoot an indie horror flick—*Mule Skinner Blues* shows a forgotten world of lonely outsiders clinging to the dream of pop stardom.

The filmmakers behind *Mule Skinner Blues*, Stephen Earnhart and Victoria Ford, came up with the interesting idea for their documentary film by keeping their eyes and ears open. They stumbled into Mayport and

left knowing they just had to come back to chronicle the hopes and dreams of the amazing people they met there.

In the end, the filmmakers help Beanie and the other people we meet in the trailer park to actually write, shoot, and edit a horror movie penned by none other than the janitor Larry Parrot. As director Stephen Earnhart explained to me: "We wanted to show people with this movie that you can just go out and do it. That was our philosophy: we're all in the same boat, we all have this burning desire to create."

❶ DO-ABILITY

Can you actually do this? If your idea is for a nine-hour-long *Lord of the Rings*–like epic in which the tree people, led by a spiky bush named Bobo and a wise wizard in the form of a willow tree named Wandalf, rise up against evil furniture makers, you may want to reconsider your plans.

The motion pictures we see on television and in theaters cost millions of dollars to make. Explosions, car chases, and trees coming to life and wrestling loggers on the lip of a cliff are all very difficult things to make seem even remotely real without trained professionals who do nothing but set up car chases or animate plants for epic battle.

Motion pictures also take a lot more time to make than they appear to—so start off thinking small and doable. A five-minute film is more than enough of a challenge! Don't worry, you'll get to your epic battle between the forest and the lumberjack one day.

❷ ORIGINALITY

Which brings us to the next consideration. We've seen so many movies and TV shows, it is very easy to slip into familiar genres and types. The temptation is to make something familiar to us, a sitcom or a movie where a little girl rescues the entire world by coming to terms with her parents' divorce and her lack of self-esteem. If your idea is just like that show you watched last week, only your main character (played by you, of course) is a surgeon who moonlights as a private eye as opposed to a lawyer moonlighting as a— Ah, forget it! We can't compete with the full-time corporate creatives whose job it is to make genre entertainment. Our version will always look cheaper, have less realistic and exciting chase scenes, and lack the multi-million-dollar star power.

If you want to get noticed working in film and video, you need to be original. But in the motion picture business, anything outside of a predictable genre is described as "art" or, even worse, "experimental." No! The horror! We wouldn't want to be *experimenting*!

Since so many people are already familiar with the different kinds of commercially made TV shows and movies, our best option is to tap into that familiarity and use genre to our advantage. Use genre to get your audience to relax into a new kind of viewing experience—the DIY motion picture. In other words, you can pretend that you are making a sitcom but then do something totally different with the setup.

Why would you want to do that? Because what we watch on TV rarely challenges us to reconsider anything about the world we think we know, or about the nature of creativity and culture. Because *subverting* genre is a great way to tell a different kind of story, to call attention to the fact that there are many stories *not* told on television or in corporate moviemaking. By playing with genre and subverting it, we realize how limiting it can be. If your actors suddenly burst into song while supposedly investigating a series of grisly murders, you are calling attention to how predictable the thriller genre is, and having a good laugh in the process.

As with all forms of creativity, the best work starts close to home. What your video might lack in slick production values and special effects, it can make up for in honesty and emotion. It is always original to make motion pictures about your life, your community, what you know. I'm not saying that you shouldn't tell stories and take viewers with you on wild adventures. I'm just saying that the way to make those adventures and stories ring true is to base them in what you know.

FORM

Indie film and video projects can take many forms. You don't have to think in terms of feature films and half-hour- or hour-length projects that might end up on NBC. You don't necessarily need actors, either. You can use puppets or dolls. You can use drawing and animation. You can eliminate the need for characters/actors altogether by, say, making a documentary in which regular people are talking about themselves and their neighborhoods. You might also want to make a motion picture that doesn't have any people in it at all and doesn't tell a story in a conventional sense. There are lots of films and videos that simply show images and actions. That might sound boring, but think of it like photography. Sometimes a single image can stand out and say more than a steady barrage of dramatic moments. When we are freed from the need to follow a story, we sometimes see the beauty and complexity of images more

Video vs. Film

WE MAY USE the verb *film*, as in "He's film-ing his movie right now," but in truth you'll most often be making a video and never see a single strip of film. What's the differ-ence? Film is the process of exposing spe-cial photographic paper to light. Film needs to be handled carefully and developed by professionals. As a result, it's expensive and difficult to edit. In contrast, video cameras are everywhere these days. Video works by turning a scene into recordable, storable data. We shoot our indie movies in video, not film, because video is access-ible and immediate and, most important of all, cheap! The biggest advantage for the budding director is that you can make all the mistakes you want with video and it won't cost you much more than a battery recharge. Don't like what you've shot? Erase the memory and shoot it again. But once you've exposed film to light, there is no going back. Long live video!

intensely. There's also the possibility of making film and video without actually shooting your own material at all. How does that work? Well, there's a great tradition of using material taped off TV or from home movies to make all kinds of really fas-cinating and weird new motion pictures.

Here's a list of some of the forms film and video projects can take:

SCRIPTED STORY For this you need a script, actors, sets, etc. By far the most ambitious and demand-ing kind of film/video project. But keep in mind that your motion picture doesn't have to look or feel like it's ready for TV or the movie theater. Scripted stories can be as short as a few minutes, and can incorporate elements from all the other motion picture forms discussed below.

DOCUMENTARY In a documentary, you set out to create a record of something happening in real life. Look around you—aren't there all kinds of inter-esting people and places in your community? Real struggle and change can be far more interesting than fiction. Say, for instance, your local grocery store is closing, put out of business by the giant Save-A-Buck that opened across the street. Might not sound like much of a story, but if you inter-view the owner of the store, it could turn out he has been in your neighborhood for 30 years after

escaping a revolution in Iran. You might just tap into a bigger and more important story than you first realized.

MOVING PICTURE PHOTOGRAPHY Call it art, call it experimental film or video, think of it like taking a picture—but the thing you are taking a picture of is captured in motion. With this kind of motion picture making, turning what is around you into emotion becomes more important than telling a story. Moving picture photography doesn't have a story—the project is driven forward by imagery. These projects can be set to music or sound effects, or you might set a series of images to a reading of a poem or journal, or the sounds of cars and trucks hurtling down a highway. Surprising contrasts can show us aspects of our lives in new ways. For instance, you might take a (moving) photo of an abandoned lot filled with weeds gently swaying in a rising sun. Then you might set that to a background soundtrack of (absent) children playing. This creates a meaning and series of emotions that are just as powerful as any story.

PLUNDER Remember plunder? After music/sound, film and video are the most plundered pop culture products. The idea here is to "borrow" from the vast amount of motion picture material already out in the world and turn that stuff into your own thing. Plunder can be part of a culture jamming project—using images we are already very familiar with in a way that changes their intended meaning. So, for instance, if you were to tape an episode of MTV *Cribs*, a show where celebrities show off their massive mansions and collections of sports cars, and replace the sound with your own soundtrack of statistics on the huge gap between rich and poor in the world, that would be a great example of culture jamming. Plundered motion pictures can also be personal, or can, through using found images from film, television, and home movies, reflect on how different kinds of moving pictures take on different contexts depending on the circumstances. They can also be very funny. You might consider merging footage you shot on your own with plundered footage. For example, you could do a *Cribs* parody in which you merge some of the *Cribs* shots with scenes praising the virtues of your terrier's doghouse and your cat's litter box. To plunder is to expect the unexpected!

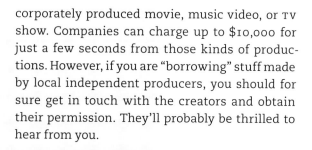

Copyright Alert

As you may have already figured out, using bits and pieces of TV shows and movies in your work might be technically illegal. Copyright is a huge, complicated subject, but generally speaking, the key here is to be creative and to fly under the radar. In other words, if you are making a not-for-profit indie project to show to friends only, then you probably don't have to worry much, even if some of the images you borrow are copyrighted and owned by a giant Hollywood corporation. But if you plan to try to sell your work, post it to the Internet, or submit it to film festivals, then you have to be more alert to the hazards of borrowing without asking.

Instead, you might want to re-create a show or movie using slightly different names and plots. That way, you are still referencing stuff we are familiar with but avoid copyright violation. Remember, parody is protected by the laws of free expression, no matter what anyone tells you. Or, if you choose to use footage from an independently produced film, you might actually get permission if you ask.

Whatever you decide on, don't even bother trying to get permission to use a clip from a corporately produced movie, music video, or TV show. Companies can charge up to $10,000 for just a few seconds from those kinds of productions. However, if you are "borrowing" stuff made by local independent producers, you should for sure get in touch with the creators and obtain their permission. They'll probably be thrilled to hear from you.

The Mechanics of Making a Movie

Now we're going to take a look at what you need to make your own motion picture. This is going to be a general overview, but it's plenty to get you started. If you want to learn more, you'll have to do your own reading on operating cameras and sound equipment, editing motion pictures and sound, working with actors (amateur or otherwise), and creating special effects. (See page 123 for a list of books and websites devoted exclusively to indie motion picture creation.)

Writing a Script

You don't always need a script, and your script doesn't have to be written on expensive scriptwriting software. For your needs, any word processing software is fine; in fact, you can write your script using pen and paper if you want. You really only need a script when you are working with a story requiring predetermined dialogue and

George Lucas Versus the Fans

IN 2002, LUCASFILM ran a contest to find the best independent films related to *Star Wars*. For devoted fans of the movie series, this seemed like an incredible opportunity: the winning film would be chosen by George Lucas himself. But the fans quickly soured on the contest. Lucasfilm decided to limit the competition to spoofs and documentaries. Those films that paid tribute to *Star Wars* by creating their own plots that spun off from the "official" story were cast aside for "copyright reasons." Said a Lucasfilm vice president of marketing: "We love our fans. We want them to have fun. But if in fact somebody is using our characters to create a story unto itself, that's not in the spirit of what we think fandom is about. Fandom is about celebrating the story the way it is."

And yet there continue to be thousands of fans who love *Star Wars* so much they feel the urge to add new twists to its plotlines. The infamous "Phantom Edit," an unauthorized version of Lucas's *Phantom Menace* film, edits out the widely hated Jar Jar Binks character and various plot overlaps. Twenty minutes shorter and some say better than the Lucas version, the Phantom Edit suggests what many of us have known all along: that some amateur fans may be just as talented as the professional directors when it comes to telling a good story. The Phantom Edit gave rise to several other anonymous edits of the film being circulated around the globe via the Internet and even handed out at conventions by rabid fans—until Lucasfilm issued a press release threat about copyright infringement.

Was Lucasfilm right to deny fans the right to re-edit their favorite movie or use the characters to make new films? How far can fans go before they are simply stealing someone else's ideas?

actors. It is possible to use improvisation instead (which means making things up as you and the actors go along), but if you have a very specific story that you want to tell, then you will need a script. Most books on script writing assume that your goal is to write for Hollywood or for television. Your script—and your story—doesn't have to follow those rules. You might be better off just going to a website with lots of movie scripts on it. Read the scripts and watch the movies they correspond to and you'll get the general idea. Remember, you aren't a professional whose every mistake adds another million dollars to the budget. You can keep it loose, spontaneous, and fun. Your script doesn't need to include every single line of dialogue, facial expression, and camera shot.

In other forms of motion pictures, from documentary to plunder, you won't necessarily use a script. But that doesn't mean you won't need lots of advance preparation.

Planning/Preproduction

Production is the industry term for the actual shoot. So, obviously, *preproduction* is the planning you do before you get out there. Yes, you can just go out and experiment, but that can take up a lot of time and not give you much in the way of results. Though it's a great idea to just muck around with your camera so you can get the hang of it, when you want to get serious about having an end prod-

uct to show to people, you'll need to put your project through what we'll call here preproduction.

Okay, you have an idea, which can be anything from a full-fledged story you've turned into a script, to a sensation you want to capture—say, the dizzying array of products in your local Save-A-Buck Grocery Center—to a documentary about how the arrival of the Save-A-Buck is forcing the local neighborhood grocery store out of business. In all cases, you need advance preparation. You don't want to obsess and ruin the fun, but you do want to think about how you are going to get your idea out of your head and into the world.

A preproduction plan involves:

1) scene shot list and schedule

2) set/setting

3) crew and actors

4) equipment (including props and costumes)

SCENE SHOT LIST AND SCHEDULE

You don't have to believe me, but this might just be the most important part of the whole process, whether you're planning a mockumentary

about repeated sightings of Bigfoot in your back-yard or a romantic thriller starring the kid in your class who most looks like Elijah Wood. Filming is always complicated, and the more people you involve—actors, crew, Dad to make a pile of his famous brownies—the more complicated it gets.

So the first thing you need is a scene shot list. This is a list of all the scenes in the motion picture you are making *in the order that you plan to shoot them.* That last part is crucial. Most movies are not made in chronological order. You make your shot list by grouping together all the scenes set in a particular place and planning to film them all in the same day. Say you are working on a documentary about the impact of the Save-A-Buck on the neighborhood. When you interview the owner of the local market, you can also arrange to shoot the neighborhood, the closed-down store, the store owner, and his family. This kind of preparation saves you from having to go back to the same location and people 20 different times.

Scene lists are also useful if you are working on a scripted story. Say you have five scenes in a graveyard in your script. Even though the scenes appear at five different points in the story (one at the beginning, three in the middle, and one at the end), you could order your shot list by setting so that you can shoot all the graveyard scenes at the same time. This saves you from having to rent the lights, gather the equipment and crew, and get across town to the cemetery five separate times. The more you know in advance about what you want to do, the more time and energy you can apply to getting what you want the way you want it.

Once you've put together your scene shot list, then you make your shooting schedule. Your plan is to make in a weekend a 10-minute movie that involves a rogue Sasquatch finally cornered in a graveyard. (Turns out he's friendly and just likes it there 'cause it's quiet and he can eat the flowers people bring... but that's not really relevant to scheduling.) So your schedule might look something like this:

SATURDAY

7 a.m.: backyard scene #1

9 a.m.: backyard scene #2

11 a.m.: front of house scene #1

12 p.m.: lunch

1 p.m.: interior bedroom scene #1

2 p.m.: interior bedroom scene #2

3 p.m.: interior basement scene #1

4 p.m.: on the road scene #1

5 p.m.: on the road scene #2

6 p.m.: on the road scene #3

SUNDAY

9 a.m.: graveyard scene #1

10 a.m.: graveyard scene #2

11 a.m.: graveyard scene #3

12 p.m.: graveyard scene #4

1 p.m.: lunch

2 p.m.: downtown street corner scene #1

3 p.m.: downtown newscaster scene #1

4 p.m.: downtown newscaster scene #2

5 p.m.: downtown newscaster scene #3

6 p.m.: dinner and wrap-up party

Now, you're probably saying: Did I read that right? Does Saturday really start at 7 a.m.? Yup, you read right, so set your alarm. Filming can be tiring, and it can take a while. Plus, if you are working outside, you want to leave lots of time available for daylight. Shooting a few minutes of your script could take up to an hour or more. Plan for delays and disasters. Allow extra time for special situations, like when your actors freak out and need to spend some "alone time" with their cosmetics.

SET/SETTING

Now that you have a list of scenes to shoot and a schedule, you need to scout your locations and

make sure you can actually be in the Save-A-Buck or the cemetery when you want to be. Remember, anything can happen. The weather can change, the security guard can chase you away, or the airplane show you didn't even know about can drown out the dialogue and ruin the whole day.

So you want to scout out your setting: check the weather, check for special events in the area that might surprise you, and, of course, check to see if you need permission to shoot there.

Getting permission can be difficult. When people hear "film shoot," they think "Hollywood" and then they think "money." Make sure to tell them that you are a student working on a school project. (Even if that's not entirely true, a little white lie can go a long way.)

DIY film and video makers often find themselves having to do things on the sly, or else come up with an alternative they can do in their backyard or basement. We don't have the money to pay for permits and rental fees. So the important thing about setting is to plan ahead: scout out where you want to shoot and determine possible problems—noisy traffic, angry security guards, nosy neighbors, etc. Come up with ways to deal with potential problems, including a plan B if you end up not being able to shoot what you had in mind. It's a good idea, for instance, to have a rain date if you are planning to film outside. If the people at Save-A-Buck refuse to let you shoot at their store, you'll have to be creative and build a grocery store aisle in your high school cafeteria.

Remember, it's only a movie! You don't want to risk life, limb, getting hit by lightning, or having a criminal record just to get your shot.

CREW AND ACTORS

Friends and family make great crew and actors. They can play your lead roles, help you set up lights, hold mics, operate cameras, and so much more. Usually you'll find lots of people willing to help just for the experience of being part of something cool like making a movie, however short or potentially amateurish.

How many people will you need? That depends on what you are doing. Say you are making that Bigfoot mockumentary. You have five characters, including the Sasquatch himself and the reporter he befriends and falls in love with. So you need five actors. You'll want someone big for the Sasquatch. Know anyone on the football team? Luckily, Bigfoot doesn't have to act too much, just moan and beat his hairy chest. The other actors, though, could use some skill. Your family and friends might have untapped dramatic talents you don't even know about. Give them a shot. Or you can try asking the drama teacher and the people involved in yet another school production of *Grease*. You can also try other schools, local college and university drama programs, and community theaters. Make a few signs and put them up. Choose your actors based on whether or not they fit the look you have in mind, their availability and willingness to put in the time (very important), and, last but not least, whether or not you think they can convincingly play a reporter who falls in love with Bigfoot.

If you are doing a documentary, then you don't need actors, but you will need a crew (of course, for *Bigfoot* you'd need both). Your crew will work your camera(s), set up the lights, hold the boom microphone, put out the snacks, keep on the lookout for strangers accidentally stumbling into the shot, and more. For an indie feature film like *Bigfoot*, you probably want five or so crew; for a simple documentary, two should be plenty. Though you want to be sure you have enough people to help out, it's a good idea to keep your team as lean as possible—remember, everyone has to be scheduled, fed, and told what to do. People hanging around the set causing a ruckus are going to distract you from directing the actors and getting the shots you want.

Throughout the project, keep your actors and crew informed about what you are doing and why you are doing it, and make sure they know if you'll need them for an hour or two hours or three days. Give them scripts and scene shot lists in advance. Your crew will be happiest if they are given at least a week's advance warning of the shooting dates, are supplied with snacks and/or meals, and get plenty of credit for their contribution in the final product.

You know what you want, but your actors just won't cooperate. Early MGM director Edmund Goulding coaches student actors for their kissing scene during a 1927 "motion picture" class.

EQUIPMENT

Making film and video can be expensive. Depending on what you're planning, you'll need at least one video camera, a tripod, possibly separate equipment to record sound (for dialogue, background noise, or both), and lights (especially if you want to shoot night scenes or indoors). Remember, Hollywood movies and TV shows are shot using millions of dollars' worth of equipment, so don't expect what you do to look as good. But these days there is a wide range of digital video cameras that are easy to use and will produce a very watchable end product. Often you'll find that you wind up using whatever you can get your hands on. So don't get all fussy and waste money unnecessarily in pursuit of the perfect gadget. There have been entire festivals dedicated to films shot on Fisher-Price cameras made in the 1980s just for kids! There are even screenings devoted to movies shot entirely on cell phones. You can make great work using almost any camera available.

If your family or someone you know has a video camera you can use, great. If not, ask around at your school—there may be cameras and other equipment you can borrow. If that doesn't pan out, ask around at community centers and youth groups and see if they have any programs aimed at helping young people make their own films/videos. If none of that turns up what you need, bigger cities will usually have some kind of film/video collective that rents out equipment at a reduced rate to members. They will also have editing computers you can rent by the hour, saving you the expense and difficulty of acquiring software. As a last resort, there are always companies that will rent you whatever you need—but they aren't cheap.

At the bare minimum, you will need the following:

VIDEO CAMERA Almost anything will do, but your best bet will be a digital video camera from the last five years or so. (Your parents' first-generation vid-cam that records on VHS isn't really going to cut it.) You want a digital video camera with light balance and a built-in mic. That may sound fancy, but it isn't—it's pretty standard. To achieve different effects and see what your camera can do, read the manual. (I know, I know, isn't there a way to just press a button and have all the info instantly downloaded into your brain? 'Fraid not.)

LIGHTS Use what's there. Don't shoot at night. Those are two excellent ways to save yourself the hassle of having to worry about lighting. For inside shots, get yourself a clip-on light fixture with a shade that you can point directly at the subject. Then you can "fill in" the set with regular shaded lamps using everyday light bulbs. Make sure you have plenty of light and that you aren't mixing light sources—which means don't use fluorescent and regular light fixtures to light the same shot. If you insist on shooting in very dark places or want a more professional look, consult the experts at your local audio/visual rental company.

SOUND Test out and try to settle for the camera's built-in mic. This will work best if you are going to do mainly close-up shots, meaning the mic is near the speaker. Or get your hands on an external mic that will plug into your camera. These can be rented, bought, or borrowed. If you are using an external mic, rent a boom—or better yet, make your own by duct-taping the mic to a broomstick or a painter's pole. Then have your sound tech hold the mic as near to the scene as possible without actually getting into the frame of the camera.

Always test your sound before you start to shoot and check it after every scene.

PROPS AND COSTUMES If you're doing a Bigfoot movie, you need to make a Bigfoot costume. If you're doing a Save-A-Buck documentary, you might want a shot full of empty, discarded boxes to symbolize the death of small business in your neighborhood. Either way, you can tell from your script what costumes and props you need. Make a list, recruit a costume coordinator (yes, give your crew fancy names—this will make them work harder), and be sure you have what you need before you are going to need it.

No matter how you get your hands on what you need, spend time figuring out how your camera works, how your sound equipment works, and how your lights need to be set up. If you are using a digital video camera, you can practice and experiment to your heart's content because you can erase as you go and your only expense is batteries. So shoot your sister on the phone, your dad making dinner, your mom backing out of the driveway. Shoot your friends, bugs crawling in the sidewalk cracks, a dog doing his business at the park. Shoot everything and anything until you are sure you know how to use your camera and won't be wasting everyone's time when you gather actors, rented equipment, and sets all in one place for the big event.

Shooting/Filming

Okay, now you're finally ready for your "Lights! Cameras! Action!" moment.

If you've done your preparations, this should be a fun process and, as they love to say, a great learning experience.

Generally, shooting is simple: point the camera and press the button. Of course, it can be much more complicated than that. Here are some things to keep in mind:

BATTERIES, BATTERIES, BATTERIES I can't say it enough. Don't run out. Lay in a massive supply.

TAPES/DISCS TO RECORD ON As in: tapes, tapes, tapes. As in: see above.

KEEP THE CAMERA STEADY Unless you're going for the I'm-so-scared-I'm-trembling effect (which has been pretty overdone), you need to make sure your camera is supported. Use a tripod whenever possible or support the camera on your knee or on a table. Also, if you are following action, move slowly and steadily in a fluid

motion; don't just walk around, or it will end up looking like your dad's recording of the family trip to Disneyland.

LIGHTING If you shoot outside during the day, you're okay. For indoor and night scenes, you may need to rent lights (see Equipment).

SOUND Your camera's built-in microphone will be okay for most situations, but if you are dealing with a busy intersection or it's windy or there is a lot of background noise, you probably want to use an external mic (again, see Equipment).

Editing/Postproduction

Editing is when you take your raw footage and order it in a way that best achieves your intended effect. During the editing process, you can move different shots to different places, cut out entire scenes, speed up and slow down images, and insert and delete dialogue, sounds, or voice-overs.

If you want to build a weird collage of moments and scenes, now is the time to speed up the shots, create strange contrasts, or add a disturbing soundtrack featuring your favorite band sped up to sound like the Chipmunks.

Editing is best done on computer. Editing software can be very simple or it can be very specialized and expensive. The cheap method is to get your hands on software by borrowing, begging, or even buying

You don't need a giant movie projector costing tens of thousands of dollars to show your movie. I'll take a digital projector any day!

Your motion picture doesn't have to be perfect. So remember:

DON'T BE PRECIOUS, and don't freak out if everything doesn't go according to plan. Enjoy the moment, try to stay as true as you can to your original vision of what you want the work to look and feel like, and it will come out great (or at least kinda okay).

YOU CAN ALWAYS RESHOOT or fix things up in the editing process.

YOUR GOAL IS TO create a conversation between you and your audience. A conversation isn't always perfect, doesn't have to look like a million bucks, and doesn't have anything to do with celebrities saving the world in under 120 minutes. What you want to ask yourself throughout this process is: how will the audience *feel* about what I'm showing them?

used or older versions of programs such as Final Cut Pro or iMovie. Then you read the instructions, spend a lot of time with the help function, and eventually get to work. (There are also film/video collectives, colleges, and even high schools that have computers set up specifically to do video editing.) The basic premise of all editing software is that you download your footage into the program and then you can cut and paste the different clips where you want them. You can also add sound with these programs in the same way—by importing sound and cutting and pasting it into the appropriate scenes. This lets you put music over scenes, insert sound effects, and add voice-overs. Editing software also assists you in creating titles and credits.

The goal of editing is to create a seamless feel so that the audience can immerse themselves in your creation. At least, that's the goal of the teams of editors who work on Hollywood movies. You might want a different feel. One of the great things about DIY motion picture making is its contrast to the slick perfection we see in movies and on television. So take it in stride and let it all hang out. If your footage is coming from the right place, it won't matter if your filming or editing is a bit rough.

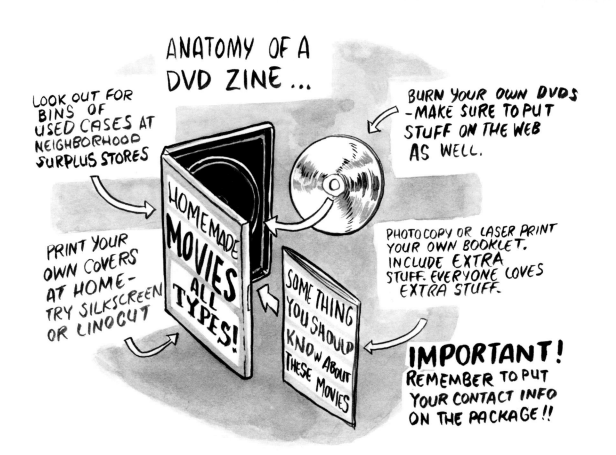

ANATOMY OF A DVD ZINE ...

LOOK OUT FOR BINS OF USED CASES AT NEIGHBORHOOD SURPLUS STORES

BURN YOUR OWN DVDS - MAKE SURE TO PUT STUFF ON THE WEB AS WELL.

HOME MADE MOVIES ALL TYPES!

PRINT YOUR OWN COVERS AT HOME - TRY SILKSCREEN OR LINOCUT

SOMETHING YOU SHOULD KNOW ABOUT THESE MOVIES

PHOTOCOPY OR LASER PRINT YOUR OWN BOOKLET. INCLUDE EXTRA STUFF. EVERYONE LOVES EXTRA STUFF.

IMPORTANT! REMEMBER TO PUT YOUR CONTACT INFO ON THE PACKAGE !!

Screening Your Work

Wow, it's showtime! Yes, definitely have a party and show the film to your cast and crew, your friends, and your family. But if you are really pleased with what you've accomplished, you should get the work out into the world. Now, the chances of your movie making it into a theater chain or onto the TV are slim, no matter how good the finished product is. But there are still ways to get your stuff seen by more people than just your friends. Here are three methods to launch your motion picture out into the indie community.

❶ INTERNET

There are many websites that exist as storehouses for motion pictures. They will let you post your short movie on their site free of charge. Obviously, you will need to convert the work to the right format—usually an .MPG or an .AVI. But after that, you can post the file to as many websites as you can find. Make sure to include a snappy description to entice potential surfers to download it, and also include your email address so that people can contact you with their feedback, questions about what you are doing, or links and notices about their movies.

Alternatively, you might want to start your own website that allows people to download

How Goldi Got to Rock:
An Interview with Paula Tiberius

PAULA TIBERIUS is an indie filmmaker who has often found inspiration in the world of rock and roll. I caught up with her not long after the release of her first feature film to find out what she'd learned from the experience.

Your first feature film, Goldirocks, *is about a girl who gets cut out of a band by the guys when she starts writing and playing her own songs. What are you trying to say about independence and creativity?*

Actually, *Goldirocks* is a film about a girl who realizes it's more satisfying to express herself through her own songs than to sleep with people who write and play songs...the guys cutting her out of the band is just a stepping stone to the epiphany. Independence is vital to creativity, and if you want to be an artist—write songs, paint paintings, or make films—you have to find your own voice and make other people look and listen. No one else is you, and you shouldn't try to be someone else.

A lot of people want to make movies. What are some of the challenges you faced writing and directing your first movie?

The biggest challenge of my first feature was writing it. I had to give up all inhibitions and fear in order to tell the story I wanted to tell. I worried that people would think it was a stupid story about a slutty girl, or that the setting was portrayed inaccurately, or that certain real-life people would recognize themselves in my characters and be upset. Compared to the agony of that process, financing, casting, and shooting didn't seem that hard. The truth is, once you can stand behind your screenplay, it's easier to do the work you need to do to get it done.

How did you get started as a writer/director?

I went to university for film theory and criticism, which basically consists of watching movies and writing about them. Somewhere in my third or fourth year, I got this overwhelming desire to do it myself. I made short films, and eventually got to travel around the world to film festivals. Then my eyes were open to what my future looked like.

What advice can you give to young would-be script-writers, directors, and actors?

Whatever you're most excited about—do THAT. Don't write because your father was a writer or act because you're trying to get back at your mother. Do what means most to you, or you'll be miserable. If you don't know what to write, or what you want to make a film about, dig deep and find the most humiliating, bizarre, or painful thing that's ever happened to you, and start there.

How much fun was it to make a movie? What's the funniest thing that happened?

I loved being on set and making the movie. What a power trip! Lots of funny stuff happened, like the actors Sasha and Greg making their fake sex noises. In the film, their two characters are supposed to be doing it wildly upstairs, and the other band-mates can hear them in the kitchen. But we only needed audio for this, so they're just sitting in the hallway pretending to have sex. It was hilarious. The whole crew was cracking up. There was so much gig-gling on those tracks, we had to slice and dice to get a proper take.

How can people get their hands on Goldirocks *and find out what else you are planning?*

Well, the DVD's almost done, but I don't have the money to put it out (oh, the joys of filmmaking!). But it's going to be cool—it's got concert footage from our film premiere party with tons of bands, deleted scenes that show a whole other subplot, director's commentary, stoner guy commentary…As soon as I sell a screenplay, I'll get them manufactured and the news will be on the website—www.goldirocks.com.

In this scene from Paula Tiberius's first feature film, *Goldirocks*, Goldi toasts her future with her good friend Lil and Rhonda, her rocker role model.

your motion pictures. If you do that, it's a good idea to include some stories about how and why you made your work. Who knows, you might just inspire someone...

❷ FILM FESTIVALS

You'd be amazed how many DIY film festivals there are that might show your work. Start with small film festivals in your community. You can usually find them by checking local arts and entertainment listings and by doing web searches. The more indie motion pictures are made, the more festivals and indie video nights there are at local schools, community centers, galleries, and independent theaters. Some communities even have festivals just for first-time filmmakers. Remember that the people putting on these festivals and special events are often volunteers. They may be disorganized and need some prodding. Send them a CD or DVD or VHS of your work (whatever format they request) and make sure your phone number or email address is very obvious on your package and on the tape or disc label. Also make sure your package is well taped up so that nothing falls out and gets lost in transit. And don't be afraid to call or drop by a few weeks later to make sure the package was received and your work is being considered. (Note: In some communities, there may be a public TV access station that also considers programming from the community; the submission process would be pretty much the same.)

❸ TRADE/SALE

As with zines, you can trade CDS or DVDS or VHS tapes of your work, or offer it for sale through the mail. To get the ball rolling, you will need to find zines, magazines, and websites that will review your work and let people know it is worth getting hold of. Send out review copies, and always make sure to include contact details and information about whether you would be willing to trade, offer the film for sale, or both. If you want to sell your work, consider keeping the price as low as possible—just enough to cover your postage and the cost of burning or dubbing. Remember, the idea is to get your movie out there!

So now you're ready to become a director, actor, set designer, screenwriter, and editor—all in one. But don't worry. We grew up editing in our minds, imagining how scenes might look, sound, or even feel if they were captured on camera and transferred from real life to the movie screen. No one knows exactly what makes a great film. But everyone knows the only way to find out is to get out there and discover how different the world looks through the lens of the camera.

Further Reading

★ *Attack of the Killer Video Book: Tips and Tricks for Young Directors* by Mark Shulman and Hazlitt Krog

Digital Guerrilla Video: A Grassroots Guide to the Revolution by Avi Hoffer

Digital Video for Beginners: A Step-by-Step Guide to Making Great Home Movies by Colin Barrett

★ *Filmmaking for Teens: Pulling Off Your Shorts* by Troy Lanier and Clay Nichols

From Reel to Deal: Everything You Need to Create a Successful Independent Film by Dov Simens

Girl Director: A How-To Guide for the First-Time, Flat-Broke Film and Video Maker by Andrea Richards

The Guerilla Film Maker's Handbook by Genevieve Jolliffe and Chris Jones

Guerilla Video Primer (VHS cassette)—how-to in the fine art of guerrilla video journalism

How Movies Work by Bruce Kawin

Inside Out by Lisa O'Brien

★ *Let There Be Life! Animating with the Computer* by Christopher Baker

★ *Lights, Camera, Action!: Making Movies and TV*

Making Movies on Your Own: Practical Talk from Independent Filmmakers by Kevin J. Lindenmuth

Moviemaking Course: Principles, Practice, and Techniques: The Ultimate Guide for the Aspiring Filmmaker by Chris Patmore

Writing Your Screenplay by Lisa Dethridge

www.channel101.com—tons of funny, obnoxious indie TV shows for viewing

www.exposure.co.uk—Internet resource for low-budget filmmakers

www.papertiger.org—nonprofit indie video collective

www.videoactivism.org—artists using video to support social, economic, and environmental justice campaigns, plus lots of resources

★ *www.youthchannel.org*—dedicated to youth-made TV and media

Do It Yourself

I SAID WHAT? Conduct on-camera interviews with your friends, family, or teachers as if you were Oprah or some other celebrity interviewer. Edit the interviews to tell completely different stories than the ones told in the interviews.

FAKE THE SCENE Re-create shot by shot a scene from one of your favorite movies using your own sets and actors.

TWO-MINUTE PHOTO Make a two-minute video with no sound, no people, no dialogue—just images from the world around you.

Keyword Search

indie/independent film/video

do-it-yourself film/video/TV

guerrilla video

Pop Music's Not Dead

It Just Needs a

(DIY) Revolution

Popular music is the soundtrack of our everyday lives. No matter in what direction the world tilts and turns, we deal with it, at least in part, by turning up the volume and pumping our tunes out of our basement speakers.

Sometimes it's great that we don't have to say how we feel. We can press play and relax, knowing that someone else is doing the work of telling the world about our emotional state for a change.

That's the essence of pop music: it's music meant to be listened to out loud (and often in public) that nevertheless conveys our intensely personal feelings. Each and every one of us secretly sings a different song in the shower, has a different desert island mix on our iPod, but the music we are so personal about is also the music that brings us together for cheesy high school dances, karaoke sing-alongs, and stadium rock concerts.

And so, pop music—sometimes awful, sometimes wonderful, but always catchy in a way that no other kind of music is—has become one of the great media of electronic mass communication. It conjures up private feelings even as it joins together millions of basement-dwelling, guitar-clutching weirdos who can't find time to do their homework or take out the trash but somehow manage to spend hours every night screaming non-

sense lyrics over the reverb of the pawnshop's cheapest electric.

Hey, we may be odd, our parents may tell us that we're going to grow out of it, but none of that matters—because we have our music. And the music tells us things about ourselves and our world that nothing else can.

You Say You Want a Revolution

Today we have the opportunity to make and broadcast our own pop music like never before. After all, this is the age of widely available home recording equipment and software, Internet radio, and file sharing—the ingredients that make indie DIY pop a growing force. If you don't like the mushy songs about love or the angry songs about being the best gangster, you can make your own music. As more and more pop music falls under the control of corporations and corporate radio stations, it's up to us to make real music that reflects our communities, our interests, and, most importantly, our times.

In other words, pop music isn't dead. It's just been drugged into a coma by the for-profit music

makers who want everything to seem edgy and radical but give us songs that all sound the same. But the spirit of pop lives on. If anyone is going to re-create, rediscover, and reinvent popular music, it will be that next generation of budding creatives—in other words, you.

So You Wanna Be a Rock 'n' Roll Star

Pop star is probably the most popular fantasy career ever. What could be more exciting than the rock and roller who burns bright, lives large, and dies at the height of his or her fame? We've heard the story so many times, we could probably act it out if we wanted to, complete with convincing lip

synching and air guitar. Unlike movie stars, who work on closed sets far away from the public, pop stars face the bright lights and the expectations of their fans. Nothing beats putting on a good show, with your audience cheering wildly, singing along, or even fainting when you play the latest hit.

But the fantasy is just that. For every Kurt Cobain or Janis Joplin who supposedly burned bright and was just too passionate and talented for this world, there are thousands more who poured their lives and hearts into the rock and roll dream and are now selling insurance or pumping gas. The fantasy is that, to succeed, all you have to do is dream the biggest dream, live the largest life. And all those *Idol* reality TV shows encourage us to believe that you can emerge from anywhere to become the next great pop star. But in truth, at the heart of great talent is great commitment to one's craft. A career in music is intense and demanding: the constant rehearsals and practice, the never-ending touring, the struggle to develop a fan base. The fantasy is different from the reality, and if we learn anything from the deaths of people like Cobain, it is that they died alone and miserable, isolated from their family and friends.

Few of us have the talent or the dedication. But that doesn't mean we shouldn't rock. One of the great things about pop music is that, as

Oliver Schroer recorded an entire album (*Camino*) while on a wandering hike with a digital recorder and his fiddle.

any karaoke fan knows, it is accessible, fun, and, though not as easy as it seems, hardly something exclusive to budding musical geniuses. After all, just about anyone can form the music chords C and G, the backbone of at least half of all the pop songs ever played. And some of the great rock and rollers of all time could barely play a single note.

So forget about screaming fans, limos, and dying young. Just get together with some friends, a few instruments, and a catchy tune in your head and see where it takes you.

What If I'm Tone-Deaf, Can't Play an Instrument, and Can't Carry a Tune?

A lot of us aren't musically inclined whatsoever. And we don't have to be. There are all kinds of ways to make music and sound. There are weekly gatherings of drum circles that hearken back to Native American and African tribal rituals. How much do you need to know to bang a bongo? (A lot to be the percussionist in an African jazz band; not so much to make a lot of noise and have fun.) This type of musical get-together is the heart and

soul of popular music—available to everyone, and part of the beat and rhythm of the community.

Luckily, very few of us are actually tone-deaf. And most of us are able to carry a tune and learn a few chords on the guitar or the keyboard. There's no reason why we can't sing and play our own songs, form a band, and otherwise express ourselves in noise. We may sound horrible at first, but hey, remember the tried-and-true saying: practice makes... Ah, never mind. It doesn't have to be perfect!

Though everything we hear on the radio tends to have lush harmonies and carefully constructed melodies, there is a whole world of different kinds of pop music that we can make and be involved in. The music we create doesn't have to sound like every other pop song out there. Here are a few different kinds of pop music that you might want to explore.

THE POP SONG We all know this one. It's the classic jingle complete with three stanzas, a repeated chorus, and some kind of guitar solo. But in the age of MP3s and CDs, there is no reason why your pop songs have to be two minutes long. In DIY pop music, the song can be a 20-minute jam or it can include a 30-second burst of feedback and screaming. It can be just about anything that joins your lyrics and music together in a way that rocks your world.

and TV, jingles from commercials, announcers at sports events, revving car engines, and snippets of songs, speeches, and sounds you might think up and create yourself—all this comes together to make a sound piece. What is it? It's not a song, exactly, though it may have a beat and even seem like music sometimes. But really, it's more of an exploration of your world and what it sounds like today.

Songwriting

So, what are you gonna make music about? From the pop song to the sound song, there are endless possibilities. (Let's say that from now on, when I use the word "song," I'm also including sampled songs and sound-type "songs.") You can make songs about almost anything. Yes, there are the classic subjects: the boy or girl you have that crush on, your sucky job at the mall, the feel of the wind in your hair as you and your pals cruise down the highway on the way to the beach. Songs have been written about those things before, and they'll be written about them again and again so long as we get crushes, have to work for a living, and don't run out of suntan lotion.

All the same, there's a lot more to make songs about than that. Songs come from some

THE SAMPLED SONG Rap and dance music are famous for "borrowing" the beats, choruses, and lyrics of other songs. This is known as *sampling*. Though some record companies have tried to stamp out this kind of creativity with lawsuits, sampled and plundered music is bigger than ever in the DIY world. You can make collage songs, too. Editing music on the computer takes some practice and some specialized software, but once you get the hang of it, you'll be surprised at what you can achieve. You can remix your favorite songs, or make your own songs out of bits and pieces of other people's tunes. Of course, if you are planning on putting anything out there that you have borrowed from another artist, you'll need to get permission first. To avoid this, you can work with music you write yourself, or just create nonsense pieces of random remix—conversation starters that ask what pop music is all about and how it comes into being.

THE SOUND SONG More and more indie creators are working not so much with music and pop beats, but with sounds. News reports from radio

emotional place inside you. They aren't usually about the history of the Hawaiian donut or the plight of the small neighborhood grocer being shut down. Music has its own unique ability to tap into feelings that can't be expressed through words or images. As a longtime amateur songwriter (I once wrote an entire song consisting of me yelling "The Leaves Are Falling!!!"), I find that my songs usually come from some emotion I can't seem to express any other way.

Which doesn't mean that your song has to be about that particular emotion. Say I'm sad because my 90-year-old grandmother has fallen ill and it looks as if she is going to pass away. I might pick up the guitar and start trying different chords and notes. I might have a lyric in my head—something about leaves falling? In the

end, I might write a song describing a walk an elderly woman takes through a park in autumn. There's nothing in there about dying or my relationship with my grandmother, but there's an emotion that suggests those things in a way that only sound and music can.

Songs almost always tell stories. But the best songs tell their story through feeling and emotion rather than characters and explanations. The feelings you evoke in a song can be happy, angry, sad, nostalgic. The key is that you *feel* what you are creating. And remember, a song can burst out of you in 20 minutes or it can take days, even weeks, to create. Just because the notes sound wrong or the chorus isn't working or you can't find the right sound for the right moment doesn't mean you should stop working on your

This Ain't No Hava Nagilah:
Every Day's a Party for the Barmitzvah Brothers

JENNY MITCHELL STARTED the Barmitzvah Brothers when she was only 15. Since then, the band has toured North America and been on the covers of magazines, and it continues to produce eccentric, fun, and totally independent music. I asked Jenny to talk to us about being young, making music, and doing it all on your own.

How old were the members of the band when you formed, and what was that like?

When the band started, me and my friends Gillian, Robyn, and Stacey were 15, and our drummer Geordie was 13 (he was still in grade eight!). It was really fun because it was really silly. We had all kinds of ridiculous instruments, like toy pianos and Zube Tubes and spoons. It was a neat experience because the more we played together, the better we got at real instruments. Within a year we had another drummer—John, who was also 13—and we were playing small accordions and bass guitars and keyboards.

When you're young, how do you get people to take your music seriously?

There's really nothing you can specifically do other than write songs that mean something to you. We had a lot of people come to our shows because they wanted to see the band that was *so young*, but then they'd see the show and realize that there was a lot more to it. If you write songs with substance, then people are bound to take you seriously.

Your band writes and records all its own music. How did the band figure out how to do all that stuff?

We were lucky because we were pretty limited. Because we didn't know how to play instruments properly, we couldn't do any cover songs, so we had to write originals. Then later, when we got better, cover songs didn't seem as exciting anymore. In terms of recording, Geordie's brother and father are both musicians, so we got to use his dad's studio, and with his brother helping us out. The songs were played "live off the floor," which means there were no overdubs, and the recording went pretty quickly. We got to make CDs and sell them almost right away. Limiting yourself and setting small, short-term goals really pays off when your band is starting out.

What advice can you give young people who want to make their own music?

Write your own songs. Playing cover songs is a hard habit to break out of, but no one will take you seriously until you do it. And if you want to record, get a friend to do it, and make the CDs yourself by hand.

How can people find out more about your music?

We have a website: www.thebarmitzvah brothers.com. We also have songs that can be downloaded at http://cdbaby.com/cd/barmitzvah.

song. Take a break and go back to it the next day. Suddenly you'll realize what's missing.

Tips for the Budding Songwriter

TAKE YOUR TIME. Rome wasn't built in a day. Neither was Pink Floyd's *The Wall*.

KEEP A MINI-RECORDER with you to capture the lyrics or melodies that appear in your head at odd moments (but not in science class, please).

GO WITH IT. When you get the urge to try out something, don't just sit there on the couch like a lump. Turn off the TV and grab your banjo!

PLAY A LOT. Often songs emerge unexpectedly when you are just fooling around with different notes or chords or lyrics. Try all kinds of different combinations, noises, and instruments. Don't worry if nothing seems to be coming together—it'll happen (see the first tip above).

BE ORIGINAL. Your songs don't have to rhyme, they don't have to have a chorus, and they don't need a Hendrix-style guitar solo.

Recording

Recording is the process by which the songs you write and play are turned into digital files that can become tracks on a CD or MP3 files or any other format used to distribute music. In the past, to record you either had to go into a very expensive studio or else you needed special hardware such as a four-track recorder. These days, few people use the four-track. You'll get better sound and save time and money if you record directly into a computer.

To do so, you need the right software, and a way to plug your instruments and microphones into the computer. (Depending on your system, this might involve a special computer card for sound and a special audio-input plug.) You'll also need microphones if you want to record vocals or musical instruments (like drums, violins, or harps) that are not already wired with a pickup that plugs directly into a computer. Anyway, there are lots of different hardware/software combinations, ranging from the pretty cheap to the ridiculously expensive. (More on this in a second.)

The most important thing to remember about recording these days is that, by using your home computer, you can record a lot of music and then edit and recombine and plunder and remix to your heart's content. Once you get used to the software, you can try out all kinds of different sounds. Computers let you easily add different drumbeats and effects like distortion or echo. Some software programs allow you to input music and then choose different instruments to

play it. With a digital recorder, you can download any sounds from the outside world that you record, and these can then be imported into your music-editing program and mixed into other music.

And of course, for those of you who like instant results—and who doesn't?—it only takes a few minutes to burn a new bunch of songs on a CD-R and give them to a friend or email them. Forget fast food—we're talking fast music.

Tracking the Tracks

A key concept to understand when recording is the idea of *tracks*. Each instrument you record (including your voice) can become a "track." So your singing is one track, your guitar is another, bass guitar is another, your backup vocals are another, and so on and so on. Most software/computer combinations can set you up to work with at least 20 or so

tracks, which is way more than you should need (unless you're composing a symphony, which might be a bit ambitious at this point).

The great benefit of recording in separate tracks is that you can hear each part of your song separately. So, if you love the vocals but the guitar sounds horrid, you can keep the vocals and just rerecord the guitar. Or you can make the vocals louder and lower the levels on the guitar so that it is just barely audible in the background. Eventually, of course, you will put all the tracks together and have a song.

When you record, generally you record one track at a time. For instance, first you might record keyboards, then guitar, then vocals. Or if you are sampling or working strictly with electronic music, you might have bass on one track, drum on another track, synthesizer on another track. All of this means that you (and your band)

PERSONALLY POPULAR:
The Music Lurks Inside Us

WHEN I WAS a kid, my parents signed me up for the obligatory piano lessons. I learned to read music, play scales, and plink out the same simple classical tunes pretty much every kid who takes piano lessons learns.

I didn't hate it, but it wasn't exactly what I had in mind.

I wanted to rock.

So I told my parents that I wanted to play guitar, not piano. Fine, they said. Before I could say "Jimmy Page," I was getting guitar lessons from a French violinist whose glass never seemed to empty of red wine.

Classical guitar lessons.

Still wasn't exactly what I had in mind.

But I had a guitar now. And after a lackluster pluck through my assignments, I would take that guitar down to the basement and spend hours trying to make its nylon strings sound electrified and badass.

Never did, but at least I tried.

Finally, around age 13, I convinced my parents that I was ready to learn a different kind of guitar—rock and roll.

Next thing I knew, I was receiving instruction from a guy in jeans and a cowboy hat who managed to infuse the cheesiest pop hits of the eighties with country-and-western twang.

Ah, thanks, Mom and Dad. Close, but not quite.

Still, after the aging cowpoke rode off into the night, I took my new acoustic steel string guitar down to the basement and turned those eighties songs into screaming-angry punk screeds.

Eventually, I was spending a couple of hours a night in the basement just pounding at guitar chords and yelling stuff. It was around that time that I wrote my first song.

It wasn't very good.

But it was mine.

will play certain sounds and song parts over and over again, sometimes hundreds of times. Of course, you can also record the whole thing live, with your band playing the song on one track. That's a lot simpler, and it can keep a tune fresh. But it severely limits your ability to edit the audio after the fact. The more technical and complicated you want to get, the more options you'll have and the more gear you'll need. But to keep it simple, record one track at a time directly into a computer. The biggest challenge is to stay fresh and excited. You don't want your band getting bored. Remember that it can take an entire week of evening sessions to record a single song.

Equipment Basics

It's easy to make music; lungs, lips, and a couple of hands to clap out the beat is all you need. But if you want to introduce some complexity into the concept, then you're going to need equipment. What follows is a short guide to the basics, not including whatever instruments you want to use (guitar, piano, viola, mini-recorder to capture the rhythmic sounds of the highway).

COMPUTER A decent computer made in the last eight years or so should do just fine. You'll also need to install a digital audio sound card.

SOFTWARE There's a wide variety of software available. If you do a Net search, you'll find recording software available for free that you can download. Try downloading and tinkering with Audacity. Then there are (possibly) more reliable programs like PowerTracks Pro Audio and n-Track that cost $30 to $50, also available for download. Finally, there are the professional software packages such as Pro Tools, which go for $300 and up. Why not start with the free stuff and, as you develop your skills and want more options for recording, move on from there? After all, you don't need to learn to play guitar on a Stratocaster.

MICROPHONES Yes, you need a decent mic! The mic is the key to recording anything not directly plugged into your computer. Keyboards and electric guitars can be fed right into the system, but vocals and any acoustic instrument like drums or piano need to be miked. Microphones can be bought, borrowed, or rented. Check out the music department of your school, local colleges, and libraries as possible sources for cheap or free

I Live with the Band!
Rocking the Duplex

How did you come to be in the band Duplex?

Well, we have been friends since we were five, and Saoirse's parents and all the people living in her duplex were musicians, so we all decided to form a band.

What instruments do you play in the band? Do you, or did you, take music lessons?
Saoirse plays the electric guitar and used to take guitar lessons. Sierra plays the piano and takes piano lessons as well.

A lot of young people might be nervous about getting up on stage and doing a show. Do you get nervous before playing a gig?

It's really funny because I [Sierra] was really nervous before our first show, but Saoirse wasn't. Apart from that, we've never really gotten nervous. Although once I did have a dream, the night before, that nobody came to our show and we forgot all of our lyrics!

Do you write songs for the band? How does Duplex go about writing songs?

Yes, we've written many songs for Duplex. Usually the songs by Duplex are about things that actually happened, so the songs we write are about stuff that involves us.

With a 3-year-old, a 12-year-old, and a 13-year-old in a band that also features various parents and friends, Duplex makes indie pop music fun for the whole family! Cover art from the Duplex CD *Ablum*, released by Mint Records.

SIERRA AND SAOIRSE are two members of a band called Duplex that also features a gaggle of professional indie musicians and a three-year-old. I talked to these two teens about what it's like being in a band and having your CD put out by one of North America's premier indie labels, Mint Records.

What are your names and how old are you?

Saoirse, I'm 13.
Sierra, I'm 12, almost 13.

Here's the band Duplex, with Saoirse and Sierra at the front. The band got its name because all the members originally lived in the same duplex house.

Duplex has recorded a CD and is working on a second one. What's the best and worst part of recording?

The best part of the recording studio is the recording part and that we're there all day, so we get to eat really good sandwiches! (We also do enjoy the foosball table and excruciatingly outdated Nintendo.) We have to admit the worst part is mixing the CD, which is truly BORING!

For more about Duplex, visit Mint Records at www.mintrecs.com.

equipment rental. Let your parents and friends know what you are doing; you would be surprised how many people have an amplifier or a microphone they never use kicking around in the attic. Unfortunately, it's hard to tell if you are getting a good mic or not. Ask the people you are renting or buying from to recommend a decent mic for an affordable price. If you happen upon one for free, try it out first. If your recording is staticky, flat, buzzy, and/or distant, it is very likely that your mic isn't up to the job.

Finding Your Vibe

Once you've got the equipment, perhaps the biggest challenge is to figure out your sound. Your sound can be anything from feedback and distortion to a pop-song sound set to a background of what seems like a full orchestra. Take the time to experiment and get a sense of the possibilities. But beware of adding lots of sound effects and relying on tons of computer-generated beats and musical instruments. Sure, it's a lot easier than finding someone to actually play a real instrument, but as much as technology makes DIY easier, no computer has yet been able to replace the feeling created by the real thing played live. In the end you want a simple sound that will highlight what this is all about: communicating

emotions to your potential audience. All the samples, dubs, loops, and sound effects in the book won't hide the fact that you didn't spend enough time working on your lyrics or your basic melody.

Playing Live

If you have written songs, figured out a sound, and are considering recording, then it's time to think about doing some live gigs. Yes, I know, this sounds daunting and even pop-star-like, but believe me, playing live is about as frightening as asking someone out on a date (it gets easier each time). Of course, just because you do it doesn't mean you're going to either be famous or find true love. So why play live? Because there's nothing like the experience of sharing your songs with other people. Because you can learn more about

how people respond to your songs in one live gig than you can in a year alone with your computer. Because it's fun. So here's a quick primer on playing your first live gig.

Finding a Venue

First thing you want to do is find a venue. Ideally your venue would be free; that way you won't have to go through the trouble of charging admission. Your goal is to get a lot of people out to your show so they can see what you can do and give you feedback. Charging a cover might keep them away. So, where to play? Schools and community centers are obvious possibilities. Local art galleries, restaurants, and clubs are also possible. They may not be willing to give you a prime Saturday night, but they might just let you have the place for free on a Sunday afternoon. Keep asking around, and

With its short, sweet, catchy pop songs, the band Paper Moon has released two CDs and built up a following while staying true to their indie ideals.

always use any connections you have—like, say, your uncle Marty who owns a downtown bistro. Of course, you want to try to keep in mind the music you are planning to play. You wouldn't book a fancy restaurant to play death metal in.

Another great option you should consider is playing a gig in someone's basement, living room, or backyard. An excellent place for a gig is wherever people can comfortably gather, where there's space for your setup, and, of course, where angry neighbors won't call the cops and complain about the crazy noise from next door.

Attracting an Audience

The audience is key; without them there's no show. The best way to let people know you are playing is word of mouth. (Unless you're planning on doing a show at your house, in which case you should make it clear that it's a private party.) Tell your friends, siblings, and parents and ask them to tell their friends, siblings, and parents. Make flyers and hand them out to everyone you know, and ask them to take a few extra and pass them on. Post messages

on listservs you might be a part of, and send a message to everyone in your email address book and ask them to pass it on. Make a poster and put it up at school and anywhere else you are known and hang out. Set up a site online in MySpace or other friend-connection sites and post information about your gig. Above all, don't stress—sometimes you are better off playing to 10 people who are really interested than 50 people who are there to talk to each other and ignore you.

Setting Up

Depending on your venue, setup might be the hardest part or a breeze. If you have a five-piece band and everyone needs mics and amplification, then you are going to have to find a venue that is already wired for live music. Otherwise, you'll need to rent such things as speakers and a mixer and find yourself someone who can adjust your live sound (the "soundman"). This is too complicated and expensive to undertake for your first-ever gig, so don't even try. A better idea is to find a way to play an acoustic set. You can still amplify your voice and instruments by using microphones and amplifiers, but if you play in a small-enough room you might not need to.

If a lot of your work is electronic based—sound and collage songs—then you might consider reducing the live element and calling the show a listening party, where you play a CD and maybe just sing or do the vocal portion live.

More and more people are making sound pieces that simply can't be replicated live. Presenting this music to a live audience may take a bit more creative effort. One possibility is putting together a slide show or video to accompany the music. This gives people something to look at while you fiddle with the keys and present your latest electronic creation.

Playing Your Set

Plan out in advance what you are going to play. Test out your sound system and make sure you sound good and can be heard from the back of the room. Also make sure that anyone playing with you knows what is going on and that you have all practiced together as many times as necessary to get your songs right. Make a set list—a list of the songs you are going to play—and follow it. Don't plan to play 50 songs. Ten songs is plenty, and if your audience want more they'll tell you, so prac-

tice an extra couple for an encore. Keep your gig to an hour or so. Remember to thank your audience for coming, to tell them a bit about where the ideas for your songs come from, and to encourage them to let you know what they thought of your music.

Thank You and Good Night

Not quite. At the end of the show, encourage your audience to add their names to your email mailing list, so you can let them know about the next performance or where they can download or pick up your music. Encourage them to hang around

Chasing Fame at the Hard Rock Academy

THERE ARE ALL kinds of schools, academies, and crash courses that promise to give you what it takes to become a rock and roll star. But it's always important to take a close look at these promises. What are they really selling?

Affiliated with the Hard Rock Cafe chain, the Hard Rock Academy shows in an advertising flyer a museum wall with a Madonna dress, a Lenny Kravitz guitar, 'N Sync's shirts, and, smack in the middle, a big *Space Available* sign. "Find out what it takes to fill this space," urges the flyer.

Don Wood, one of the Academy's founders, describes it as a "boot camp where would-be performers can see where they stand." Teenagers gather for a week or two and work on their singing, dancing, and general look. They get to record a CD single. When they're not playing pop star, they're touring the Hard Rock Cafe's memorabilia collection or taking a limo ride to their very own wrap party. "It's an opportunity to see what the music business is all about," Wood enthuses. "How to create an image, how to market, what goes on behind the scenes."

Yes, all of that is probably a lot of fun (expensive fun, though, since it costs thousands of dollars for just a week). But what the Hard Rock Academy sells is the *feeling* of being a rock star. After all, anyone can enroll in the Hard Rock Academy. You don't audition to get in—you just pay the hefty fee. The Academy is more like one of those reality TV shows where you dress up to look like a pop star and then get to meet a real one at the end. "What we're trying to do is give them an appreciation of what it is to be a star," says Wood. In other words, at the Academy, everything is set up to make you *feel* like a star, but no one ever tells you the truth about how unlikely it is that you will ever be a pop idol. In fact, there are no music lessons, no instructions on writing song lyrics, nothing about all the hard work that goes into being a great performer and entertainer— let alone a great musician.

And yet, as the Academy's flyer makes clear, the empty space on the Hall of Fame wall is waiting to be filled—by your gold record. So what's the lesson here? Avoid any course or camp that implies it will make you a star. Playing music isn't about the hoopla and the limo ride to the pretend Grammys. It's you and a few friends in the basement, eyes shut, amps cranked, ready to rock.

and talk to you, too. Keep in mind that you'll have to put away your equipment and clean up the venue, and that your host might not want you to hang out for another two hours talking to your friends. So no matter how tired you are and happy that your first gig is over, be considerate and make sure you clean up and clear out so that you'll be invited back.

Getting Heard

There are, of course, other ways to get your songs heard than playing live. First off, though, let me just say that there is absolutely nothing wrong with simply jamming in your basement and never playing your songs to anyone. Ever.

But most of us want more from our music and sound making. We want to be part of a culture that constantly invites us to create and put ourselves out there. Still, even if you are a great, talented musician, you'll find that a lot of doors are closed to you. There are so many people trying to get attention, it often comes down to whom you or your parents know, or how much money you have to promote yourself. That doesn't mean it's

hopeless, it just means you have to work harder to get yourself heard above the babble.

To start with, forget about hearing your songs on commercial radio. Don't even waste your time. Commercial radio includes the all-hits radio stations, the "alternative" rock stations, the easy listening stations. Owned by private companies and dependent on ad dollars, they will rarely play a song or group that isn't already popular, lest people lose interest and tune out. Occasionally, stations may have some kind of local bands competition and play songs by area acts. This is great if you are doing commercial pop rock and hoping to get attention from a major label, but if your work isn't mainstream, you may be out of luck.

Otherwise, if you want play on the radio, see if there are any noncommercial stations in your area. Traditionally, noncommercial radio comes

The dance-punk-pop quintet You Say Party We Say Die know how to get attention!

in two forms: public radio, such as Canada's CBC and the United States' NPR, and college radio stations that feature students and members of the local community doing shows on everything from death metal to salsa to ultra-left-wing politics. If you are going to try to get heard on these kinds of stations, you need to find out which shows play your type of music. If you are a sound sampler and there is a late night show on your local college radio station dedicated to that kind of work, then obviously you want to send in a CD to that show's host and/or producer. Check out the website, find the names and contact information, then send in something for airplay. When you send in your CD, be sure to include contact information, a biography that talks about who you and your collaborators are and what your sound is like, and information about any upcoming gigs and where people can buy or download your songs.

Radio Here, Radio There, Radio Everywhere: Beyond FM

Competition to be heard on public and college/community radio is intense. Don't be disappointed if you don't get any airplay. There are other growing forms of radio, many of which are entirely indie and open to playing just about anything. These include:

INTERNET RADIO—people broadcasting live radio just on the Internet

PODCASTING—radio shows that are available for download on people's iPods or phones

PIRATE RADIO—low frequency radio that is broadcasting to a relatively small number of people. (In the next chapter I'll talk about ways to start your own radio station.)

Again, Internet searches and asking around in your community will help you find the various DIY creators who are working in independent

The Death of Napster
and the Future of File Sharing

BY NOW, NAPSTER is old news. But when 19-year-old Shawn Fanning started his online file trading service in 1999, Napster revolutionized how people get their hands on music around the world. At its height, 60 million or so users were joyously downloading free music. Like the mimeographed or photocopied newsletter, it was simple, brilliant, and provided people access to the songs they wanted when they wanted them.

Napster was short-lived; it didn't take long before the service was awash in lawsuits and complaints. There were good arguments to be made about lost royalties and copyright infringement. But saying that Napster was about people stealing music missed the point. What Napster gave us was the potential for anyone in the whole world to create a song and make it available, if they so desired, for free download to anyone else in the whole world.

From the point of view of an indie music creator, file trading is not some evil monster stealing your money—it's your best friend. The truth is, you aren't trying to make a profit in the music biz, you are just trying to communicate. The best way to do that is to get your music out there easily and at no cost to either you or the listener. File sharing lets you do that. Napster is now a for-profit service, but it is still possible to share and trade files through a variety of different online methods.

radio and could be excited about playing your songs.

Finally, a great way to get your music out there is to post it on websites for download. There are zillions of sites that showcase new indie music. Send them tracks and ask their webmasters to put you in their listings. Always be sure to include information such as your email address and the URL of your own website in case interested fans want to find out when your next gig is or how they can get more of your music. You can also have your tracks playing when people visit your MySpace site or its equivalent.

There are so many ways to make music and get it out there. The whole manner in which we listen to pop music is changing, creating amazing opportunities for people like you and me to start supplying our lives with our own soundtracks. So what are you still reading this for? Get playing!

Further Reading

Basic Mixing Techniques by Paul White

★ *Beginning Rock Guitar for Kids* by Jimmy Brown

★ *Booking a First Gig* by A.R. Schaefer

Digital Home Recording: Tips, Techniques and Tools for Home Studio Production by Carolyn Keating

The Everything Home Recording Book by Marc Schonbrun

★ *For Those About to Rock: A Road Map to Being in a Band* by Dave Bidini

★ *Forming a Band* by A.R. Schaefer

Guerilla Music Marketing Handbook by Bob Baker

Guerrilla Home Recording by Karl Coryat

Guide to Home Recording on a Computer (DVD) by Roger McGuinn

How to Write Songs on Guitar by Rikky Rooksby

Label Launch: A Guide to Independent Record Recording, Promotion, and Distribution by Veronika Kalmar

★ *So You Wanna Be a Rock Star?* by Stephen Anderson

homerecording.com—info on recording, mixing, and making your own equipment and instruments

recordingwebsite.com—tips, articles, training

Do It Yourself

(RE)ARRANGE IT Record the lyrics to your favorite pop song. Rearrange the song's lyrics and melodies. In other words, give the song a new tune and even a new meaning by changing it around. Take a sad song and make it happy. Take a heavy metal song and turn it into bubblegum pop.

DID YOU JUST HEAR WHAT I HEARD? Take a mini-recorder out into the world. Record various noises: a bus pulling away, birds chirping, ambulance sirens, two people chatting. Play your recordings back at home, listening to how different sounds record and how background sounds can have their own beat and emotional tone. Make a sound piece out of your real-world recordings.

KEEP ON ROCKING IN THE FREE WORLD See a live band. A lot of us almost never see live music, but you can learn tons just by watching other people play. So get out there and check out a band—any band.

Keyword Search

home recording

DIY/indie music

songwriting

community radio

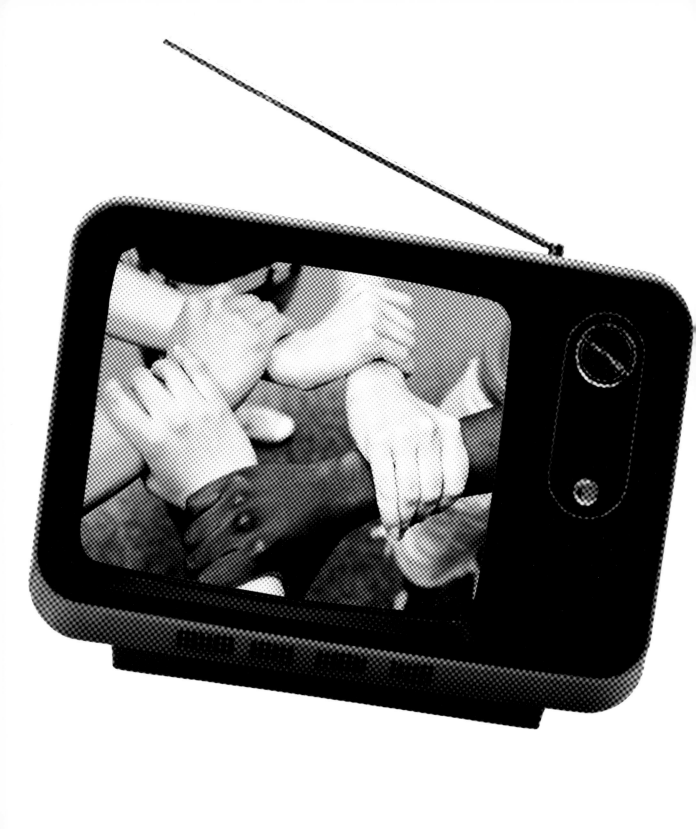

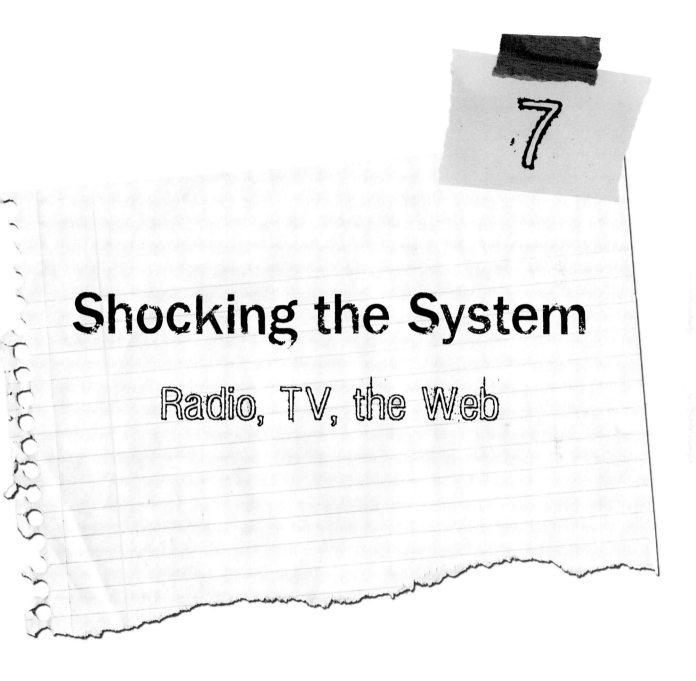

7

Shocking the System

Radio, TV, the Web

RADIO, television, and the Internet. All three of these electronic media are ways to distribute your music, movies, words, and pretty much anything else you can come up with. DIY creators don't have access to satellite or cable television, we can't get songs or sounds onto corporate radio, but we can start our own TV channels and radio stations and websites. Just like Fox, WB, and Disney, we can create networks that give people quick, easy access to entertainment content. But unlike the networks owned by giant corporations, we don't have to choose our content based on how many ears or eyeballs it'll attract to the millions of dollars' worth of ads we're expected to sell.

Internet, TV, and radio are distribution networks. That means they aren't artistic or creative entities on their own, but places people go to get access to pop culture. So when we talk about these three ways to distribute (or broadcast), we are really talking about creating new places where people can go to discover different kinds of independent pop culture. The goal of this chapter is to get you thinking about not just making pop culture but also starting your own distribution network. You think you can't have your own radio or TV show? Sure you can! In fact, you can have your own channel.

Independent distribution is about making connections, giving people access to different kinds of pop culture, and setting up communities of user-participants—people who will both tap into what's on your network and make their own stuff that you can broadcast. If you put as few roadblocks as possible between you and the potential users of your network, you'll be amazed how

quickly your community and the whole DIY project can spread.

People who love indie pop culture but don't necessarily have the passion or desire to write or film or play music often turn to helping other creators get their work out there. They hear a song or see a movie they think is great, and they want others to find out about it. The best thing about being a distributor is all the great work you'll be exposed to and the fascinating people you'll get to meet. As the go-between for different creative endeavors, people will be searching you out, sending you CDs and movies, and cheering you on. Plus, you get to decide what you want to play or show or display on your network. You're in charge, you're the tastemaker—what could be better?

Pirate Radio:
Sound Outlaws Sail the Airwaves

Pirate radio sounds pretty wild. After all, pirates are criminal outcasts who roam the rough waters in search of boats they can waylay and rob. Surely that doesn't have anything to do with radio, does it? Well, if you ask corporate radio stations and most governments, they'll tell you that anyone who broadcasts "illegally" is an evil buccaneer every bit as bad as the dreaded thieves of the high seas.

But over the last 20 years or so, independent pop culture creators have become proud of the "pirate radio" label. After all, if playing songs and talking on the radio is illegal, then those who believe that the airwaves can and should be free are happy to be called pirates. They're pirates cruising the radio waves, taking over people's ears and giving them more to listen to than talk radio, classic rock, and the same so-called "alternative" pop songs played over and over again.

The pirate label also comes out of the actual history of radio. In order to avoid getting arrested for violating laws against independent

Does this young man look like an outlaw? Low-power radio broadcasting is easier than ever, thanks to advances in technology, but public access to the airwaves is tightly restricted.

broadcasting, people have, over the years, run DIY radio stations from boats. Having a radio studio in a boat meant that you could move up and down the coast, making it hard for anybody to trace your signal. And if you were far enough out to sea, you might even be in international waters, which left you free of any country's rules about who can and can't broadcast. A great example of waterborne pirate radio was the Israeli station Voice of Peace. Floating off the coast of Tel Aviv and broadcasting in violation of Israeli law, the station promoted peace in Hebrew and Arabic to Palestinians and Israelis from 1973 to 1993—20 years of sending messages of hope and reconciliation. There are still floating radio stations out there, many of which prefer to call themselves "offshore" broadcasters. But whatever they call themselves, they'll always be pirates at heart.

Now, all this is probably sounding pretty illegal. But really, most people who do independent radio broadcasts are left to their own devices and ignored. Pirate radio is considered harmless fun unless you upset the big radio stations by broadcasting with enough power to steal their listeners or advertisers. There are countless examples of small broadcasters who are never noticed or hassled by "the Man." In the small town of Merritt, British Columbia, for instance, a guy broadcasting under the name Bleek did a show for several years (see page 154), and was even featured on national Canadian television, without ever being told to stop by the authorities.

These days, as different technologies become cheaper and more widely available, there are many options for starting your own radio station or radio show. There's an entire new movement of pirate radio broadcasting out there, inspired by the groundbreaking activism of the pirate station WTRA, which was founded to serve the inner city of Springfield, Illinois, in 1986. It became known as Black Liberation Radio, and its story, though not its signal, spread around the U.S. and influenced the likes of Stephen Dunifer, whose Free Radio Berkeley movement was one of the best-known attempts to spread the idea of independent radio in America and around the world. Springfield's WTRA broadcast for years, until its ongoing popularity attracted the attention of the U.S. government. The station was eventually forced to shut down, but pirate

You Gotta Fight for Your Right to Party: AMATEUR RADIO, A CASE STUDY

IN THE EARLY part of the 20th century, all kinds of people were broadcasting; radio was practically ruled by amateurs. But because there were so many radio stations all broadcasting on the same channels and potentially canceling each other out, governments stepped in and made laws. The various wavelengths were divided up. In the United States, the Act to Regulate Radio Communication of 1912 determined who could use what radio frequencies. Corporate interests got the best bands, government the second-best, and so-called "amateurs," that is, normal people who were broadcasting to their communities, got one single wavelength, a frequency that was so limited in its coverage that broadcasting was almost pointless. Hey, at least they got something! It wouldn't be long before the amateurs were drummed out altogether.

By the 1950s, the governments of North America were awarding radio stations almost exclusively to corporations. As quick as you can say "monopoly," various corporations bought radio stations and started making money by showcasing the popular entertainments of the day, which were sponsored by other giant corporations that paid handsomely for the privilege. Today, with a few exceptions, the public airwaves are owned entirely by corporations.

Over the last 50 years, people have been responding to corporate control of the airwaves by once again starting their own radio stations. A lot of the time the government regulators simply turn a blind eye to amateur broadcasters. It is very possible, and in fact a fairly regular occurrence, for pirate radio stations to broadcast—for a week or five years—without anyone minding at all. Often the governments and corporate radio stations never even notice. It is possible to broadcast with a low-power transmitter to a small community without ever interfering with anyone else's signal. Even though governments in countries including Britain, the United States, and Canada generally refuse to issue licenses to individuals who want to engage in low-power broadcasting, there are plenty of empty frequencies for you to quietly occupy.

Today's radio is a classic example of what happens when corporations are given exclusive rights to distribute pop culture. Luckily, new technologies and the Internet are slowly challenging the corporate world's domination over what we get to hear.

Life before iPods was...well... awkward. A keen radio amateur trolls the airwaves with a homemade antenna while milking his prize cow!

radio continues to grow, echoing the answer one of WTRA's founders gave when asked how people could support his station: "Go on the air! Just go on the air!"

Low Frequency Broadcast

This is the traditional pirate radio format. Basically, with this format, you are becoming a broadcaster just like the local rock station. Ever seen the classic teen angst movie *Pump Up the Volume?* In it, Christian Slater plays a rebellious high school student who decides to start a radio station in his basement. The station becomes wildly popular with the students. So, naturally, the authorities get involved and have to quash the broadcast. In the end, the Slater character broadcasts live from a portable transmitter he sets up in his car, frantically monologuing to the last even as the cops close in!

Okay, the movie is over-the-top dramatic. Truth is, you'll be lucky if you can get 20 people to listen to your broadcast, let alone your entire high school. (Unless you attend one of those schools that broadcasts its own station during lunch hour over the PA system.) But the movie does give you a sense of how easy (and complicated) it is to set up your own broadcast network.

The first thing you should understand about radio broadcasting is the business of frequencies.

Basically, radio waves can be sent out on different frequencies, which correspond to the numbers on the dial of an old radio. An AM radio dial will show frequencies from 535 to 1605 kilohertz. These frequencies are all the channels you can broadcast in on AM radio. But there are other frequencies in which you can broadcast too, frequencies that are not supposed to be used by commercial broadcasters because they are reserved for everything from military to amateur or "ham" two-way communications. Every frequency could potentially carry your broadcast, provided it isn't being occupied by a bigger, stronger signal than you can put out.

How strong your signal is depends on the power of your equipment. Everything you need to be a radio pirate can be bought at an electronics store or ordered off the Internet. There are even entire home radio broadcasting kits available. You need a transmitter (also known as a transceiver—a transmitter and receiver in one unit), which is the piece of equipment that broadcasts radio waves. You'll also need a microphone, which plugs into the transmitter and sends your voice to the airwaves. As you can see from the diagram on page 153, the transmitter gets hooked up to your CD player, your computer, or even your record player.

RADIO

FM TRANSMITTER

RECORD PLAYER

TAPE DECK

MICROPHONE

TO ANTENNA

MIXING BOARD

COMPUTER FOR PLAYING DIGITAL AUDIO FILES AND FOR RECORDING YOUR SHOW.

Make a list of the equipment you need, then start finding out what you can buy, beg, borrow, or otherwise acquire. Learning which equipment to get and what kind of broadcasting (AM, FM, or two-way) it will allow you to do is your first big challenge. (You'll want to do a lot of reading and get others to help you. Check the Further Reading at the end of this chapter for books and websites that can help you choose the right gear.) Getting the equipment and learning how to use it is your second challenge. If you can't afford to buy, you'll have to search around. Ask friends, neighbors, parents. Check the Internet for people selling or giving away used stuff. Ask local colleges with radio broadcasting courses and/or college radio

stations if they have any old equipment lying around from a recent upgrade.

Setting up your station means finding a suitable space. A radio setup doesn't need to occupy an entire room. If you have a decent-sized bedroom, do it in there. A basement is also a good spot. A (safe) rooftop that has electricity and shelter from the elements is ideal—but also a pretty rare find.

Remember, how far your broadcast can go depends on how powerful a transmitter you get, how good an antenna you have (your antenna attaches to your transmitter), and where you are located. If you set up on the 20th floor of an apartment building in a big city, you'll reach

Bleek on the Block:
Merritt Free Cast Radio

MERRITT, BRITISH COLUMBIA, population
7,000. An unassuming small town hours
from the nearest city. Hardly the sort of
place you would expect to find a pirate
radio station. And yet that's where Bleek,
an indie rock fan, ended up living and starting his own pirate radio broadcast.

Originally from Seattle, Bleek has lived
in Merritt since 1994. In 1995 he introduced zines into the area with the publication of various ongoing projects, including
his zine *Speck*. In 1998, Bleek followed
this up with the introduction of Merritt's
first and only pirate radio station, Merritt
Free Cast Radio (MFCR for short). Bleek's
MFCR microcast radio transmissions were
nothing spectacular. While the region's two
or three commercial radio stations offered
up their usual mix of local news, oldies,
and new country, Bleek spun indie pop rock
songs never before broadcast in Merritt.

"I just thought I would do it until I got
some kind of reaction," Bleek tells me
after my phone call wakes him from a day
nap. "I'm not really sure what kind. I got
quite a bit of good feedback from people.
Unfortunately, nobody lived close enough to
be able to hear it. It went for two to three
blocks or so."

Every night for almost a year, Bleek was
broadcasting an illegal radio show that

barely extended past his own driveway.
All that energy expended, and for what?
Why even bother? But Bleek sees it a
different way:

"My idea of proper radio is everyone
would be doing this, transmitting, and
then we'd have a real choice . . . things that
wouldn't occur to you that you were going
to hear. I think that's where radio ought to
be. It should be always changing."

At the best of times, Bleek's microtrans-
mitter couldn't have broadcast more than a
couple of miles. His highest listenership on
any given evening was probably something
like 20 people. On some nights, there
may have been nobody listening at all. But
Bleek was happy with his year-long pirate
radio broadcast.

Even if Bleek only reached a few people,
he figured it would be worth it. As he
explained to me: "I did it because I love
the music and was hoping that it would
inspire somebody to try it, to go out there
and do it."

Build it yourself! In the 1920s, almost anyone could build their own radio. Here, a boy listens to a shopkeeper's instructions on radio assembly.

more people than if you broadcast from your parents' basement in the suburbs. At the same time, the more crowded and populated the place you want to broadcast to is, the harder it will be for people to pick up your signal.

Hello, this is the Voice of Suburbia broadcasting to you live from my parents' basement...

Amateur Radio Dos and Don'ts

★ **DON'T** spend too much money on a setup. And remember: expensive new broadcasting equipment will get you nowhere if it is hooked up to a cheap antenna.

★ **DO** scrounge around at garage sales, swap meets, and on the Internet for equipment no one is using.

★ **DON'T** jump into a high-powered FM frequency that will disrupt other stations or bring the attention of the authorities. Keep things simple by broadcasting small and local in a way that isn't likely to attract attention.

★ **DO** find someone in your community who is into pirate or ham radio and ask them for advice and assistance. Also, many communities have ham radio clubs for amateur radio enthusiasts.

Internet Radio: Around the World and Right Next Door

Many pirate, corporate, and community radio stations now broadcast online as well as over the airwaves. The idea is that, although the airwaves can usually only reach a local community, an online broadcast could potentially be heard by the whole world. Anyone with high-speed Internet can listen to your broadcast. There are also those who choose just to broadcast online. In other words, you can have a radio station without all the expense and hassle of having to set up transmitters and antennas and possibly being accused of breaking the law of the land in the process.

Internet radio works with streaming technology. This is the same kind of technology that lets you watch videos online. You can download and install the broadcasting programs fairly easily

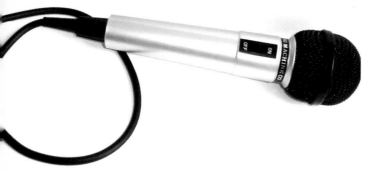

and usually pretty cheaply. (As I write this, there are a variety of options, including Shoutcast free streaming software package, Pirateradio.com, Andromeda, and the SAM Broadcast program. No doubt there will be many others, so search online to see what other options there are before you make your decision.) Once you've got your software installed, you pretty much just need a microphone that can plug into your computer so you can be a live DJ. You might also have a CD player plugged into your system or a bank of MP3s so you can play tunes for your audience.

Internet radio is relatively easy to set up and pretty inexpensive, because you can do everything from your computer. But this kind of broadcasting is also somehow distant. Who are your listeners? Well, potentially the whole world. That's a lot of pressure! There's something special about broadcasting to a very specific community—you know them and they know you. *That* is the appeal of local radio. As well, anyone in range can tune in to your radio broadcast, but the potential audience for Internet radio is limited to those listening online. Also, even if your audience could theoretically be in the billions, your actual audience might be pretty small since the Internet is jammed with millions of sites offering streaming music and movies. In the end, as with low-power radio, your regular audience

will probably be your friends and their friends—the people in your community who know what you are doing.

Generally, if you want to build an audience for your broadcast, it's a good idea to start small and local by focusing, say, on the doings of your high school or your area's music scene. Internet broadcasting works best if you have a really specific topic that will attract an audience because no one else is doing it (such as a weekly broadcast on zombies or Sri Lankan food). If you fill a niche and cover something no one else is covering, people will take notice and want to listen. So online radio can still serve a specific neighborhood, though part of the fun is imagining that people all over the world are paying attention to you.

Internet Radio How-to

You need: a CD player, recording and editing software, microphones, an audio mixer, a digital audio card, a dedicated computer with encoder software, and a streaming media server.

Here's how it works:

★ Once your audio card is installed in your computer and you've got your hands on recording software (see the section on recording music in chapter 6 for more on this), you can upload audio into your computer and store it.

★ The encoder software, which you can buy or download for free, converts and compresses your audio into the streaming format you need to broadcast.

★ The compressed audio is sent to a server that stores websites. This you have to pay for—but if you or your parents or your school are paying for high-speed service, you might already have access to space on a server with streaming capability. Of course, you also need to set up a website (see later in this chapter).

★ Finally, the server sends the audio data stream over the Internet to the player software on listeners' computers. You are now broadcasting to the entire world. (Or at least to the two people out there who know what you're doing and managed to tear themselves away from their video games to check it out.)

Podcasts

Podcasts are prerecorded radio shows you upload to a website. Your listeners can come around and download them whenever they want. Think of a podcast as an online audio zine—an opportunity to introduce the world to who you are, what you like, and how you think.

The podcast format got its name because of the practice of downloading prerecorded radio shows

HAM RADIO VS. PIRATE RADIO

THE GOVERNMENT SETS aside frequencies for amateur radio, sometimes called "ham radio." Ham radio, though fun and cool in a retro sorta way, is not really broadcasting. It is more like the kind of radio that truckers use to communicate with each other. Ham radio operators usually talk to each other or to a small group in two- or three-way conversations. They broadcast on AM bands that most radios in our homes can't access. To listen to ham radio you need a special radio receiver or scanner that can pick up what is known as shortwave radio. So ham radio, which you still theoretically need a license to practice, is more like a club of people who enjoy communicating with each other in a very specialized way than it is an opportunity to get a particular message or song out into the world. At the same time, ham radio can teach you a lot about radio broadcasting, and battery-operated ham radio broadcasts have been known to come in handy at times when the electricity is down, leaving email users and the big broadcasters unable to get any messages through.

Radio Tips Part 1

★ Record a sample and play it back to your-self. Check the levels. Can you hear your voice? Is the background music too loud or too quiet? Is there a weird buzz coming from somewhere?

★ Identify yourself several times throughout the course of your broadcast. Say who you are and where you are and how people can reach you.

★ Say what you've been playing and where your listeners can find more of the same, especially if you are showcasing indie artists.

to Apple's portable music player, the iPod. (Note: iPod is just a brand name; other companies also make these powerful little devices.) The benefit of the podcast is that you can listen to the radio show you want while on the bus, walking around, or even working out. You can also download and listen to podcasts on a desktop or laptop, or any kind of portable MP3 player, including some cell phones. Which means you don't have to have an iPod to listen to a podcast, only access to a computer with an Internet connection.

Podcasts are sort of a cross between radio and other kinds of sound recording. The equipment and technical knowledge needed would be the same as for Internet radio and for making simple recordings using a computer. Instead of the live streaming you would do for radio, with a podcast you would convert your recording to MP3 format and put it up on your site.

Though podcasters often make it seem as if what they are doing is live radio, of course it isn't. This is both the good and the bad of podcasts. You can prepare them in advance and release them for anyone to download whenever they feel like it. Also, even people with a slow connection can download a podcast, though it might take them a while. At the same time, a podcast isn't live, so if you want that live radio feel or if you want to talk about stuff happening that day, the podcast wouldn't be the right format.

Some radio aficionados use all three of these indie radio formats. This is pretty great if you are the listener: if you're in range, you can tune in through regular radio; if you are working on a computer with high-speed, you can tune in online through live streaming; and if you want to listen to the show later or bring it along on a trip, you can download the podcast and save it for when you're ready.

Radio Content

So, DJ, what are you going to play? Or say? Or perform? Starting your own radio station might seem like a really fun idea, but it's also a commitment. After all, your listeners are depending on you. Independent radio can be a forum for new music, for local news and events, for everything from comedy to politics to personal discussion. It can also be all of the above. You don't have to stick to any particular format the way mainstream radio does. You can do whatever you want, which is the exciting thing about indie radio.

But for your show to be successful, it needs to be a real alternative. If all you're doing is playing that week's pop hits, there's not much point, is there? As well, if you are playing corporate-owned pop music, you are probably breaking copyright laws. Remember, radio stations pay the music

labels for the right to play the stuff you are giving away for free.

That doesn't mean you can't play music. There are websites where bands and independent record companies make their music available for indie radio to play for free. And you can always play the music or sounds you have recorded yourself, or local bands in your community who give you permission to play their stuff.

Searching out the alternatives will keep you out of trouble and make for much better radio. But when I say alternatives, I don't mean swearing a lot and doing your best Howard Stern imitation. Yeah, you can push the boundaries and say whatever you want, but watch out for those raunchy jokes: your mom, your priest, or your neighbor might be listening. (And remember that you have the right to free speech, not the right to be obscene or degrade others.)

Whether you are planning to play music, talk, or present some kind of prerecorded documentary, think about what's missing in your local community, what people might want to hear that isn't available. Think about what *you* want to hear; if you're bored, probably everyone else is too!

A great way to get started is to follow your own interests. If you're a movie fan, maybe you want to broadcast an alternative take on the movies. You could do a weekly roundup of independent film and video, complete with clips from the

film soundtracks, interviews with creators, and updates on film festivals and screenings. Or maybe you want to do something more diverse; maybe you want to cover anything and everything going on in your community. Occasional broadcasts featuring interviews with people you've seen around town but never spoken to might make for pretty great radio. After all, everyone's got a story to tell, from the homeless guy who collects change on the corner to the butcher who's been in the same location for 40 years to the dry cleaner who just moved into the neighborhood after emigrating

from Vietnam. Or, hey, maybe you just want to focus on the happenings at your high school. Why exactly was the principal fired from his last job? Will this be the year the hockey team wins the regional championship? Does anyone other than you even care?

Keep in mind that one of the best things about radio is that it is a medium for sharing. Not only are you sharing other people's songs and stories with your listeners, but you can also invite other people to share your network and host their own shows on your station. Invite friends, family, and members of the community to broadcast their own shows. This will get your station tons more attention, particularly if you are organized and divide up the duties. If you're doing a station focused on indie pop culture in your area, for instance, you can have different hosts do different shows on everything from music to zines to online activity. This means all kinds of people involved in all kinds of DIY pursuits will find out about and want to listen to your show.

Staying on the Air: Broadcasting and Other Challenges

To start, you'll want to set yourself the challenge of broadcasting a one-hour show every week. Pick a time when you will always be free so you are on air the same time every week and your listeners get

used to checking out the show at that specific hour. Make sure you post on your website when you'll be broadcasting. If you're doing a podcast, the same rules apply: post a new show every week on the same day at the same time so that people know when to go back to get the latest installment.

Now that you're into the swing of things, you can start lining up other people to also do shows. While it's okay to have guest DJs and commentators, you only want to recruit those who are going to commit to doing a weekly or monthly show so that, again, you can put the entire schedule up on the Web and your listeners know when open-mic freestyle rap hour is happening and when the weekly hour on recycling in your community goes to air.

If you keep your listeners informed about what's coming up, and if you get as many people from the community involved as possible (by interviewing them, playing their music, inviting them to email in their opinions), then you'll soon find your station taking on a life of its own and acting as a connection between friends and neighbors. You'll also find people you don't know stopping you on the street and pitching their idea for a great four-hour special on their basement lizard-and-snake terrarium.

Radio Tips Part 2

★ Mix it up. Don't just talk for hours and hours. Plan to play music and snippets from the soundtracks of films, and have live or prerecorded interviews.

★ Be prepared. Organize everything in advance. Your listeners won't be impressed if you flounder around looking for a song to play or a story to read. If you are going to have guests come into your studio, make sure to remind them the day before to come in 15 minutes before you actually plan to put them on the air. Write down a list of questions you want to ask them.

★ Recruit a friend to help. It can be pretty difficult to play music, cue up a sound clip, welcome a guest, and chat away to the unseen masses all at the same time. Get a friend to be your producer (be sure to give him or her plenty of props) and things will go more smoothly.

★ You might not have the technology to put phone calls live on the air, but if you have broadband Internet access, you can take emails and read them out when they come in. This is a great way to connect with your listeners.

★ Practice makes perfect. Try running through a bit of the show before you broadcast. Think of some witty things to say on your topic, jot down notes, reminders, jokes. But don't write out an entire script—you don't want to sound like you're reading.

Thanks for staying with us, folks, the parents are out to dinner and Voice of Suburbia is about to rock your world like it's never been rocked! But first, a message from our sponsor, my next-door neighbor and budding poet Sarah. Sarah, take it away...

Indie TV

Yes, it's possible to have your own low-range television station. In fact, in many parts of the world independent television broadcasting is thriving. Here in North America, however, such television is pretty rare. Very few of us have seen or have access to indie television.

Why? Well, most of us get our television through either cable or satellite. These are both closed systems that lock out indie or pirate television broadcasts. Pirate radio is possible because most of us get our radio either over the airwaves or off the Internet. Both of these routes are accessible to the independent creator, who has no access

to cable or giant satellites launched into space for the purpose of beaming down ESPN.

So what does that mean for budding TV producers? Well, I gotta be honest with you: Pirate television is a very difficult thing to pull off technically. As well, in most Western countries it's illegal to broadcast television without a government-issued license.

Right now and for the next few years, the best way to do indie television is to upload a pre-recorded show to the Internet and make it available for download. People can download episodes of an ongoing show and watch them on their computers (sort of like the video version of the podcast). For instance, when a group of teens started the Backyard Wrestling Federation (see page 165), they videoed their wrestling bouts and then uploaded them to their website as a weekly show they called *The Friday Night Massacre*. What they did is different from posting a single video for download. The BYWF *Friday Night Massacre* was a regular "broadcast"—one that the audience came to expect. In other words, it's more like television because it appears in episodes. It's not live TV, but it's probably as close as we are going to get right now. (And very little of what we watch on television is live anyway.)

Currently, the other option is to post regular video installments to a video clearing house site

such as YouTube. Once you join the site, you can upload video and specify what categories you want it to live on in the site. Then you can send an email around, letting people know that your show is up and running. Again, regular installments will be what keeps viewer interest. (Note: YouTube and other video storage sites are also a good way to get one-time film and video projects out into the world. And if you're hoping to sell your work, you can just put out a trailer…)

Hopefully in the near future two things will happen that will open up TV broadcasting considerably. First, Internet data transfer speeds will continue to increase and we'll be able to stream video feeds the same way we can now stream audio. That way, when we want to see what's on TV, we will be able to choose from millions of broadcasts from all around the world.

Second, digital cable will replace conventional broadcasting. Digital cable will mean that there will be no limit on how many shows a subscriber could potentially have access to. That's because, unlike with conventional broadcasting, you don't have a limited number of on-air frequencies available. Once digital cable is the norm, we hope government will start requiring cable distributors to give more channels over to the community for broadcasting shows made by individuals and local groups.

Whatever happens, technology is developing quickly, and over the next 10 years it will become easier and easier to do indie live TV.

Making TV

Let's assume that we are pretty much limited to two kinds of DIY television: posting shows to websites, and becoming involved with a local cable community access station and possibly contributing a show to their channel. Cable community access is different in every city and town. Usually, cable providers are required by law to provide community access channels—two or three channels produced locally and open to anyone in the region. Some of these channels accept proposals for new shows via a random lottery or some kind of review board that picks the best ideas. Others have their own stable of shows that are generally imitations of the talk shows, news shows, and other fare that fill up the daytime schedules of network TV. So, depending on how your community cable access channel functions, you may or may not be able to get involved in the creative side of making TV. It's worth checking out, and there may be opportunities to learn more about what goes into making television, but most likely you won't get the freedom you would from just doing it yourself.

So, let's focus on making TV for online distribution.

From a technical perspective, you will need pretty much the same equipment and skills that we discussed in chapter 5. So, you need a video camera, video editing software, and things like lights and microphones. Again, see the Moving the Picture chapter for more details.

In terms of creative content, the various options include documentary, collage/plunder, and fictional scripted drama or comedy. But television has always been more immediate than other film and video media. It airs daily or weekly, and is often done on the fly, without elaborate scripts or lengthy edits. What makes a television show different from a movie is that your audience expects a rougher, more off-the-cuff experience.

So, you want to give your show a vibrant, live, "happening right now" feel. One way to do that is to put up new episodes on a regular basis. Plan to put up a new show once a week or once a month, and let your audience know that they can keep coming back for more. Having a regular broadcast schedule not only develops your audience but keeps the tone immediate and fluid. When you're

The DIY Full Press:
BACKYARD WRESTLING

THE BYWF (Backyard Wrestling Federation) was a deceptively simple idea. In 1998, three guys started filming matches, thinking up roles and dramas, and uploading a weekly wrestling show every Friday evening to their website. Dumping stuff on the Net is hardly an innovative concept these days, but there's a first time for everything, and this group of college students with part-time jobs as waiters and gardeners figured it was pretty damn cool that they could have their own wrestling show and find an instant audience in the thousands.

"I do it just because it's fun," Kris Verri (a.k.a. Dylan Foxx), one of the founders of the BYWF and a regular performer, explained to me when I talked to the backyard wrestlers. But Verri also admitted something else: "Every single one of us has had or has a dream of maybe one day becoming a WWF superstar."

A former backyard wrestler turned sideline showgirl whose stage name is Jasmine gets fan emails from around the world. Though shy and admitting to feeling embarrassed when her coworkers discovered the site, Jasmine goes to the trouble of applying makeup, fixing her hair, and slipping into a gaudy outfit just to walk up and down the sidelines—efforts that will make up a minute of footage on the show, at best. Like Kris Verri, she doesn't do it

for the money. And she has no illusion that backyard wrestling will bring her fame or fortune.

Since the formation of the BYWF, backyard wrestling has exploded; there are now hundreds of backyard wrestling shows online around the world. When I talked to Ken Flatt, a 24-year-old student from England, he told me he had been a backyard wrestling fan for about two years. "I later found the BYWF, which totally blew me away," he explains. "FULL SHOWS! I really admired the creativity these kids put on."

Not long after seeing the BYWF, Ken was inspired to start his own wrestling troupe. "I am working on my own federation as we speak. I have been getting lots of advice on how to go about doing things and getting shows up together. My friends and I are having a lot of fun just acting and being in front of the camera."

Ken tells me that he hopes to be the "only active wrestling federation in the U.K., even if we are a Backyard Circuit."

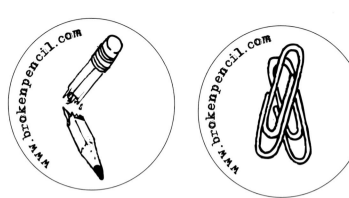

doing a half-hour show every week, it's going to have a totally different feel than a video piece you've been working on for six months.

You'll need concepts for television shows that can be done quickly and with relative ease while still ensuring that the thing is watchable. The obvious contender is some kind of talk show. You can invite your friends, people from the community, and even politicians and performers (who'll do anything to be on TV) to come and be your guests. The great thing about an open format talk show is that it lets you include everything from politics to sports to entertainment—whatever you feel like covering. The disadvantage is that your show might become unfocused and all over the place, alienating your potential audience.

You might want to consider having just one particular topic as the focus of your show:

SPORTS Doesn't have to be backyard wrestling. You could do a show on skateboarding, on parkour/free jumping, on soccer—whatever you're into. Get out there in the community and interview local leaders of the sport. You could even cover a variety of sports, profiling alternative or extreme sports that local people are doing in your area but that don't get any attention in the media.

ARTS AND ENTERTAINMENT A show that features local bands. Or invites local and emerging writers to read their stories and poetry. Or a show that every week screens a collection of indie film and video from your community and around the world. A mix is also possible, with a video by a local band followed by an interview followed by a short story reading followed by... You get the idea.

COMEDY/IMPROV While it's pretty difficult to put together sitcoms and dramas on a weekly or even monthly basis, a show focusing on comedy or improv sketches like the kind you sometimes see on *Saturday Night Live* is doable. But only if you're funny! You and your collaborators could do monologues, sketches, improv scenes, and otherwise yuck it up.

NEWS Ever complained about what gets reported on in the nightly news? Well, here's your chance to provide your own version of events. But keep

Promote yourself: these simple drawings featuring the Broken Pencil URL and the tools of the DIY trade were turned into buttons to be sold and given away. Buttons are a great way to remind people to visit your website.

in mind that you'll need to come up with your own slant; no one wants to hear you reporting on stuff that happened last week and has already been covered by your local network news. Since you obviously don't have the resources of CNN, I'd suggest starting small by covering what's happening in your neighborhood.

PLUNDER It can be a lot of fun to tape clips off TV and then edit them to say and show something totally different from what was originally intended. Televangelists, TV talk show pundits, celebrity whiners, and, of course, politicians are all excellent subjects for this kind of treatment. This doesn't have to be heavily edited material—sometimes the stuff people actually say and do in front of a camera is the funniest of all.

The Technical Deets on Internet TV

What you are doing is preparing a podcast that offers video and audio instead of just audio. This means you follow the same steps already discussed in this chapter under the headings Internet Radio How-to and Podcasts. Again, the principle is to input your show from your video camera to your editing software and then upload it to a website as, probably, an .MPG file, which your viewers can download at their leisure. Got all that?

Don't Sit So Close, You'll Go Blind! DIY TV Hints

★ Don't do it all yourself. You'll burn out. You need collaborators to help you work the cameras, recruit guests, lug equipment, and generate ideas. TV is a team effort.

★ Start out slow. Try to do a show every second month. Once you get the hang of it, you and your team can ramp up production to monthly, weekly, even daily!

★ Come up with simple sets that you can easily store (or convert back to the family room) and use for every episode. You don't want to have to re-invent the wheel every time.

★ Avoid ideas that require a lot of writing, acting, and rehearsing, or special effects. Save that stuff for your movie.

★ Mix up the visuals. TV is a visual medium, so you want to keep your audience's eyeballs glued to the screen by incorporating lots of different visual information in the form of as many short clips as you can jam in there.

At its best, TV is immediate, live, hectic, and even a bit crazy. Embrace the insanity, don't try to control it. The best way for your show to stand out

izens to interact with each other in a manner that is democratic (because everyone with access to a computer has equal access) and popular (because the Internet shows that when people have true opportunities to create, they can and will be very involved).

The Internet is your portal to the world of indie pop culture. It's the first place to go when it comes to looking for an audience for your creations.

Internet as Distributor

We've already talked about using the Internet as home base for your radio show, TV show, videos, music, and writing. Basically, if it's pop culture, the Internet can distribute it, call attention to it, or otherwise promote it. But there are other things you can do with a website that I want to get you thinking about. Your site can be many things at once, including a blog, a chat room, or even an online arcade.

and make an impression is by you letting go of the reins of control; in other words, do the exact opposite of what the networks do. Get out of the way by letting your guests and friends take over. Now *that's* reality TV.

Websites

By now you've probably noticed that the Internet comes up a lot in this book. That's not a coincidence, because the Internet is the freest, most accessible way to distribute indie pop culture. No wonder I keep going on about it. Easy to use, available around the world, and not yet subject to the same kinds of laws that regulate radio and television, the Internet is a revolution in people-driven pop culture. Whether it's sharing a reaction to a tragedy, a new twist on dating, ways to find out about cool new bands, or the best means of mastering a video game, the Internet allows cit-

Indie artist, writer, and cartoonist Sherwin Tija uses a blog to keep people in the know about his many projects.

BLOGS, WEBZINES, EDIARIES *Blogs* are sort of a cross between a zine and a diary, except that they are online for anyone to read. The point of having a blog is to rant, rave, and otherwise spout opinions about pretty much whatever you want. There are blogs about saving the environment, blogs about rock music, blogs about dating, blogs about traveling... You name it and someone is blogging on the topic. There are lots of websites that will host your blog for free; all you have to do is register and start writing. But you might also want to have a blog on your own site as a way to get people interested in your music, or videos, or upcoming self-published book.

Webzines are zines that you publish online instead of as actual paper mini-magazines. Some zine publishers will have both a paper zine and a website with online content.

Ediaries are just what they sound like—online diaries that let you post your daily, weekly, or monthly life story. But be careful, anyone could be reading this stuff, including the people you are writing about. There are even cases where people have been fired from their job for complaining about the boss online.

Why do a blog or ediary? Because it's a great way to explore your thoughts and feelings on whatever subject you choose to write about. It's also the kind of place where you can try out ideas on people who are just as excited as you are about pet ferrets or reading vintage Nancy Drew books. Many popular bloggers go on to turn their musings into zines, books, films, and other projects.

CHATS/LISTSERVS *Chat rooms*, as you probably already know, are online discussion groups where people go to talk about everything from their favorite television shows to their experiences battling eating disorders. Though there are many chat rooms, there is always room for more discussion. Your website might be a great place to host a chat room, which will not only attract people to your site but also let you create a forum for topics that are not being discussed as much as you would like. Yes, let the chat room for recovered nose-pickers be born! A chat room can complement an online radio or television station dedicated to, say, local indie artists by giving people from the 'hood a place to post announcements of gigs, new releases, art shows, zine fairs, and anything else that's going on out there. A good example of a website that has a huge chat room component is www.televisionwithoutpity.com, which reviews popular TV shows and provides a chat area for each show.

Listservs are email based, though they often have a Web component. The idea here is that you sign up on a website to receive emails from anyone else on the list who wants to communicate to the group. Listservs tend to be more focused because they come in the form of emails you choose to have delivered directly to you. Generally, a listserv serves a specific group with a specific interest. I'm a member of a listserv that discusses publishing independent arts magazines (because I'm a magazine publisher). Emails about magazine distributors, cover design, and working with writers come in daily. There are also community-based listservs. An example is free-cycle (www.freecycle.org), which has chapters in various cities in North America. Freecycle members live in a particular area and post notices of stuff they have to give away free for pickup, or request stuff they would like to get for free (within reason, usually). The result is a great bit of community building. Listservs are fairly easy to run,

and, as with chat rooms, the software for building one is widely available for free download. From the perspective of a pop culture creator, listservs can be really handy because they go out instantly to a group of people who have all indicated that they have an interest in, say, podcasts about local bands. So when you have that new podcast ready to go up, you can send an announcement to everyone on the listserv. Or if you need advice on your project, you can post a request for assistance.

DISTRO MAIL ORDER Mail order websites aren't just for giant companies. The beauty of the Internet is that it is accessible to everyone. Yes, you too can start your own indie online Sears or Amazon. But, naturally, it will only work if you are distributing what can't be bought elsewhere—independent DIY creations. In DIY, people simply call all those tiny CD or zine or book distributors *distros*.

A distro works like this: You know a lot of people making interesting indie stuff (including yourself) and you want to take on the project

Micro but Proud: PROFILE OF INDEPENDENT DISTRIBUTOR/ PUBLISHER JOE BIEL

PORTLAND, OREGON'S Joe Biel has been self-publishing zines for over a decade and has now entered the world of video making, all the while co-running a zine distribution business and book publishing project called Microcosm Publishing. I caught up with Joe to get a sense of what's involved in being an independent distributor and publisher.

Joe, you run an online independent distro outfit. What kinds of things do you distribute and how does it work?

I'm one-fifth of Microcosm Publishing and Distribution. We primarily sell zines and zine-related books through mail order around the world. We also distribute radical T-shirts, stickers, buttons, posters, videos, and patches, and have been doing so since 1996.

How did you get started as a distributor?

My roommates worked day jobs and I delivered pizzas at night, so I needed a hobby. I contacted people who made interesting things and started dumping my own money into the project. Eventually it grew beyond myself and now we have an office and are closing in on 1,500 titles.

You're also an independent book publisher. Can you tell us more about that?

Four years ago, I needed another hobby. I always feel like I can do more for the community, so when I saw people who should have books published, I eventually took steps to do that. Most of our books aren't published to make a profit for us, rather to get the books out into the world.

What's the hardest thing about what you do?

We get a lot of emotionally impacting mail that criticizes us. It's mostly from people making incorrect assumptions who don't understand what we do. Generally, the complaint is that we are "too big," or should or shouldn't publish/distribute this or that. Many people take the liberty of getting personally insulting as well. That'll be the thing that eventually stops me from doing this altogether.

Any advice for young creators trying to get their DIY zines and comics and books and videos out into the world?

You really have to work hard, and it is like having a second job. It's not glorious, but there are moments where it all makes sense. Refine your work until you are proud of it. Be confident in what you are doing but open to criticisms while still being prepared to close the door on someone that is being disrespectful of you. It's a hard line to toe that I'm still learning 10 years later.

Find out more about Joe and Microcosm at www.microcosmpublishing.com.

of helping them get it out there. An indie distro site features a list of stuff for sale: zines, videos, T-shirts, buttons, CDs, books, whatever you want to make available. You can set your website up so that visitors will select from all the stuff you have on offer and click "buy now." You'll be notified by email of the order, which you can then pack up and send out. Again, there are free or cheap software packages that will help you create an online store. The big risk, of course, is that the customer never pays you. Generally, you should probably wait for them to send you the check before you send them the product. Or you can set up your site to take credit cards using a company like PayPal. But this is complicated, and you should probably just start small and see where it takes you.

You can also act as a clearinghouse for free indie pop culture distribution by offering free downloads of videos, TV shows, radio shows, PDFs of zines, and stories.

Depending on how much stuff you have on the site and how much you are selling or giving away, a distro can be a huge amount of work or a fun hobby. It's up to you how big you want to make it and how much time you want to put into it. Successful indie online distribution usually focuses on one particular kind of activity—distributing lots of zines, for instance—rather than trying to handle every possible DIY pop culture project out there.

HOSTING YOUR OWN VIDEO GAMES An indie video game is a great feature to post on your website. They'll come for the free game and stay

On www.secretfunspot.com you'll find retro-culture galleries galore! Toys, horror, dime-store curios, and more. This site is a great example of an indie website merging with an individual's passion for weird stuff from the past.

for...whatever else you have up there. Believe it or not, tens of thousands of people are actually making cool video games completely on their own. Why? Because the games produced by the big companies are often anti-social, overly violent, and expensive. Why else? Because it's fun. A great example of an indie game is N, a 2-D action game in which you are a ninja trapped in a world of well-meaning, inadvertently homicidal robots. This free game has 500 levels and features software that allows players to make their own levels and submit them to the site to be added to the next version of the game. N was made by Raigan Burns and Mare Sheppard, who spent about 150 hours working on it after work and on weekends. Yes, you too can make your own video game!

What Makes a Good Website?

So the Internet is key to your indie pop culture efforts. It is the cheapest way to reach people around the world. You can not only showcase your songs but also run a chat room about indie songwriting and sell your CDs—all online in the same virtual space.

That said, there are a lot of websites out there that just don't seem very effective. With so much to look at, why should we stop at your site? Here are some ideas for making a good website that will bring your pop culture endeavors to the attention of your thousands of cyber-visitors:

★ Decide what your website is about. If you have recipes for vegan gravy, postings of your friend's short videos, a blog about pets, and several pictures of you and your friends at a local amusement park, then you are probably going to confuse people. If they are confused, they will move on. Try to keep your website focused.

★ Content is key. Visitors want to know that what you have on your site is fresh and original. Put the content front and center—no one wants to have to click through all kinds of filler first. Also, be sure to update your content as often as you can. That way, readers will know that if they come back to the website, they will find fresh material to enjoy. Remember that, as discussed throughout this book, the best indie pop culture is stuff that comes from you and your life in your community.

★ Keep the design simple. Leave all the flashy fireworks to the corporate types. You don't want to tie up people's computers with fancy dancing animations. Yes, your site should look slick, but keep it simple and quick to load. Once your site is designed, get your great-aunt Pearl to navigate through. If she can figure out how to get onto your online radio broadcast, then you're set.

★ Be interactive. Give your visitors lots of opportunities to be involved by posting their own opinions, offering up content, or responding to other people. Think of your site as a forum—a place for conversation, not just somewhere for people to go to see how great you are.

Invade Your Space!
Ediaries and Webcams

Colin Moser grew a community out of a Chia Pet.

"Using a webcam, I actually grew a Chia Pet—as seen in TV *Guide*—online," this 26-year-old Edmonton Internet aficionado explains. "People loved it. They came every day."

With his webcam pointed at a Chia Pet (a ceramic item stuffed with seeds that grows a plant in the shape of an animal), Moser attracted thousands to his website. It's a simple example of how a little creativity can go a long way towards getting people to notice your pop culture creations.

They come for the webcam Chia Pet and stay for the blog, the music, and the movies.

Moser used what he learned from the Chia Pet experiment about the "different ways there are to get people to go to a website" to start an online community meeting site. On his own site— chiaweb.net—he has stopped growing Chia Pets in favor of positioning webcams inside and outside his house, allowing sightseers to check out the view as they please. He also has games, jokes, and galleries of photography.

"I don't know why I do it. It's just a stupid thing," he says of providing webcam views of his house.

But Moser is hardly alone in putting up webcams that reveal his personal space. There are thousands of webcams pointed at people's homes, and probably three times that many text-based ediary sites where total strangers can read about the lives of people they've never met. This too is a new kind of pop culture creativity that can not only attract people to your site but also be a unique way to communicate who you are and what you're about.

Online ediaries and webcams have gone from being a faddish craze to another way of entering the world of DIY pop culture. Visit such sites as myspace.com, facebook.com, pitas.com, diaryland.com, www.angelfire.lycos.com, or opendiary.com and you'll find thousands of daily detailed

confessions. The diaries range from the upsetting (confessions of a girl struggling with an eating disorder) to the cliquish (lots of info about some guy's friends) to funny musings about everyday life.

Why put your life on the Internet for public consumption? A big part of it is about wanting to have a place where you can express yourself creatively. It's also fun to find out that others are connecting with what you have to say. "About once a week someone responds to what I've written," explains an ediary enthusiast named Angela. "Positive feedback spurs me on to write more. It's a huge motivational factor and actually makes me feel more free to express myself in any way I choose."

Getting Heard or Seen

At the end of the day, the distribution of indie pop culture is about connecting with an audience. As with everything you do, you will need to promote your broadcast or distro, whether you are online, over the airwaves, or both. People can't check it out if they don't know where to find it!

So, here are some ideas for getting people's attention.

FORM A COMMUNITY If projects are centered around neighborhoods and communities, they are more likely to attract support and contributions. So invite people into what you are doing: have meetings and fundraising parties, host panel discussions and workshops. Don't just sit in your basement and plot! Of course, it's also possible to form long-distance cyber-communities of like-minded folks. To do that, you'll want to visit related chat rooms and listservs, set up pages on sites like MySpace, and basically do everything you can to let people know what you are up to and how they can get involved, regardless of whether they live halfway around the world or halfway around the block.

ESTABLISH AN ONLINE PRESENCE Even if you aren't into the Web thing, you should have a website. It can be barebones simple, just what you do and why you do it and, most importantly, how people can contact you to find out more. As more and more of the world goes online, people's first reaction these days is to do a web search for something. If you aren't on there, you aren't connecting to the ever-larger number of people who pretty much do everything online. So start a simple site and send its URL to all the search engines, and ask everyone you know to link to your site.

ADVERTISE If advertising didn't work, then Coke and McDonald's would have been out of business a long time ago. Of course, you don't have billions of dollars, but make up some photocopied flyers and posters and leave them at your school, at community centers, and at indie book and record stores. You could also make a small ad for your project and offer to trade with other websites, zines, and pirate radio stations: you'll run their ad if they run yours.

BE A GUERRILLA MARKETER Use your creativity. Hang a banner in a busy urban area, stage a spectacle, call the press, spray-paint your car. If you see an opportunity, take it!

It's one thing to make a great short movie or record a great song; it's another to get that work out into the world so that people know it exists. Distribution is a big part of any DIY pop culture project. You can make a big difference in your life and to the lives of others by creating a space where people can access original artistic material. So don't just sit there reading this book. You're live! On the air! The world is watching!

Further Reading

DISTRIBUTION

www.microcosmpublishing.com—good example of an indie distributor of DIY culture

www.zinestreet.com—list of zine distributors, stores, and libraries in North America

RADIO

Pirate Radio Stations: Tuning in to Underground Broadcasts in the Air and Online by Andrew Yoder

A Popular Guide to Creating a Community FM Broadcast Station by T.J. Enrile

Rebels on the Air: An Alternative History of Radio in America by Jesse Walker

Seizing the Airwaves: A Free Radio Handbook by Ron Sakolsky and Stephen Dunifer

★ *http://radiodiaries.org/handbook.pdf*—Download a handbook on recording your own radio diary.

www.lpam.net—low-power AM radio broadcast how-to

www.soundportraits.org—Click on "education" for advice on recording stories for the radio.

www.tranquileye.com—collection of material about Canadian campus and community radio, micro and pirate broadcasting, and community networking

www.transom.org—info on making your own radio

TELEVISION

Videofreex: America's First Pirate TV Station and the Catskills Collective That Turned It On by Parry D. Teasdale

CREATING YOUR OWN WEBSITE

www.htmldog.com

www.htmlgoodies.com/primers/html

www.mcli.dist.maricopa.edu/tut

www.webmonkey.com/frontdoor/beginners.html

www.w3schools.com

www.yourhtmlsource.com

CREATING YOUR OWN VIDEO GAMES

www.tigsource.com—an independent gaming website

CREATING A PODCAST

www.podcastingnews.com

★ *www.teenpodcasters.com*

Do It Yourself

GO ONLINE FOR YOUR MEDIA For a week, only listen to online radio and watch online television. What are the differences between online media and the news and entertainment shows on television and radio channels? What's the same? What could you do better?

EXPOSE AN INDIE ARTIST! Find a band, a book, a zine, a website, or an indie video game you think is really great that not enough people know about. Take two weeks and do everything you can to get people interested in that DIY pop product. How much effort is it to get people to check out something new? What strategy seemed to work the best?

MAKE A PILOT A pilot is a prototype show for a television or radio series. In this task, the goal is to come up with a proposal for a series. You'll need an idea, sample scripts, and descriptions of the set and the actors/hosts. Pretend your friend runs a TV or radio station and ask her if she's ready to order 10 episodes. Could you take your idea and turn it into an actual show? What seems like it would be the hardest part of doing a regular series?

Keyword Search

pirate radio/television

blogs/blogging

podcasts/podcasting

zine distribution

community broadcasting

indie/DIY video games

IMAGE CREDITS

Ink splats throughout: © Kirsty Pargeter, www.sxc.hu, reprinted with permission

4 and 5: © istockphoto.com/Izabela Habur

8 and 9 (bottom): Courtesy of *Broken Pencil* magazine

9 (top): © Cathy Kaplan, www.sxc.hu, reprinted with permission

10/11: © Eirin Henriksen, www.sxc.hu, reprinted with permission

12: © Lorianne O'Grady, www.sxc.hu, reprinted with permission

13, 36, 53, 76, 101, 125, 147: © A. Hulme, www.sxc.hu, reprinted with permission

15 and 50: © Cecilia Alegro, www.sxc.hu, reprinted with permission

15: © Ilja Wanka, www.sxc.hu, reprinted with permission

17: © istockphoto.com

17 (background): © Clinton Cardozo, www.sxc.hu, reprinted with permission

18 (Imre Szeman): © Maria Whiteman

19: © Linden Laserna, www.sxc.hu, reprinted with permission

21: © elvis santana, www.sxc.hu, reprinted with permission

22 and 146 and 163: © H. Berends, www.sxc.hu, reprinted with permission

24: Gutenberg. Perry Huston Collection, Prints and Photographs Division, Library of Congress, LC-DIG-ppmsca-07359

25: Courtesy National Archives and Records Division. Photograph number 558283 "Accordionist in a polka band ..." July 1974
  Documerica: the Environmental Protection Agency's Program to Photographically Document Subjects of Environmental Concern, 1972–1977
  Record Group 412, Records of the Environmental Protection Agency 1944–1999
  Special Media Archives Services Division, National Archives, College Park

26 (top): Wandering minstrels, 1869. Prints and Photographs Division, Library of Congress, LC-USZ62-68923

(bottom): Jukebox factory, 1942. Farm Security Administration—Office of War Information Photograph Collection, Library of Congress, LC-USE6-D-003053

27: © istockphoto.com/Sebastien Bergeron

28: © Tory Byrne, www.sxc.hu, reprinted with permission

29: Circus poster, 1899. Prints and Photographs Division, Library of Congress, LC-USZC4-5226

30: H.G. Wells. George Grantham Bain Collection, Prints and Photographs Division, Library of Congress, LC-DIG-ggbain-21351

32 and 154: © Arno Enzerink, www.sxc.hu, reprinted with permission

35: © Bruno Watson

36: © istockphoto.com/Todd Harrison

38 (top): © sanja gjenero

(background) © Herman Chan, www.sxc.hu, reprinted with permission

41: © istockphoto.com/Camilo Jimenez

43: © Joe Ollmann, *The Big Book of Wag*, published by Conundrum Press

44 and 181: © istockphoto.com/Kirsty Pargeter

45 (Vinay Menon): © Andrea Witmer

46 and 179: © Marcus Beltman, www.sxc.hu

(ink splat) © tijmen van dobbenburgh, www.sxc.hu, reprinted with permission

48 (Stay Free): Courtesy of *Stay Free* magazine

50: © Kevin Abbott, www.sxc.hu, reprinted with permission

52: © istockphoto.com/Guillermo Perales Gonzalez

54: © David Ritter, www.sxc.hu, reprinted with permission

55: © blue sky, www.sxc.hu, reprinted with permission

56 (Friendly Rich): © Ilia Smirnov

58: Courtesy National Archives and Records Division. Photograph number 278195 "Computer Room—Christopher Kraft's personal copies" File Unit: MA-6 Photo CCK's Personal Copy (Christopher C. Kraft)
  Record Group 255: Records of the National Aeronautics and Space Administration, 1903–2002
  National Archives Southwest Region (Fort Worth)

59 (*Ripe*): Courtesy of *Ripe* magazine

60 (*The Andy Brown Project*): Courtesy of Andy Brown

61: Courtesy National Archives and Records Division. Photograph number 556664 "Advertising along the walls of a subway platform ..." April 1974
  Documerica: the Environmental Protection Agency's Program to Photographically Document Subjects of Environmental Concern, 1972–1977
  Record Group 412, Records of the Environmental Protection Agency 1944–1999
  Special Media Archives Services Division, National Archives, College Park

62–63 (Beige CD and poster): © The Beige, reprinted with permission

62 (shark): © Bill Davenport, www.sxc.hu, reprinted with permission

65: © istockphoto.com/Benoit Faure

66: Courtesy National Archives and Records Division. Photograph number 530736 "Douglas Fairbanks, movie star, speaking in front of the Sub-Treasury building, New York City, to aid the third Liberty Loan" April 1918
  Signal Corps Photographs of American Military Activity, 1754–1954
  Record Group 111: Records of the Office of the Chief Signal Officer 1860–1982
  Special Media Archives Services Division, National Archives, College Park

68: Courtesy of *The City of the Birds*

70 (Emily Pohl-Weary): © Walter Weary 2002

71: Courtesy of *Kiss Machine* magazine, reprinted with permission

(top) artwork © Sonja Ahlers, (bottom) artwork © Mark Connery

74–75: © Jacob Boyd, www.sxc.hu, reprinted with permission

78: © istockphoto.com/Murat Baysan

78 (background): © istockphoto.com/Kristen Johansen

79 (*Found*): Courtesy of *Found* magazine

82 (*Cornflake Rebellion*): Courtesy of *Cornflake Rebellion* magazine

83 (left, *Found*): Courtesy of *Found* magazine

(right, Davy Rothbart): © Dorothy Gotlib

85 (right): © istockphoto.com/Steve Luker

87 (Ansis Purins): Courtesy of Ansis Purins

88: Courtesy of *28 Pages Lovingly Bound with Twine* magazine

90: © istockphoto.com

92: © Judy MacInnes, Jr., reprinted with permission

93: © istockphoto.com/Shelly Perry

94 (left): Thomas Paine, 1793. Prints and Photographs Division, Library of Congress, LC-USZC4-2542

(right): Martin Luther 1882. Prints and Photographs Division, Library of Congress, LC-USZC4-6894

95: Benjamin Franklin. Between 1763 and 1785. Tissander Collection, Prints and Photographs Division, Library of Congress, LC-DIG-ppmsca-10083

96: © Tim Conley, *Whatever Happens*, published by Insomniac Press

100: © EMiN OZKAN, www.sxc.hu, reprinted with permission

103: © istockphoto.com/Mat Barrand

106: © istockphoto.com/Joshua Blake

108: © David Ritter, www.sxc.hu, reprinted with permission

109: © istockphoto.com/Paulo Ferrao

110: © Colin Nixon, www.sxc.hu, reprinted with permission

112–113: © istockphoto.com/Daniel Gilbey

115: Film students, 1927. National Photo Company Collection, Library of Congress, LC-USZ62-106955

(bottom) © Pam Roth, www.sxc.hu, reprinted with permission

117 (camera): © istockphoto.com/Paul Wilkinson

(ufo): Jorge Bermudez, www.sxc.hu, reprinted with permission

118: Movie theater projector, 1958. US News & World Report Magazine Photograph Collection, Prints and Photographs Division, Library of Congress, LC-DIG-ppmsca-03112

120–21: Courtesy of www.goldirocks.com

122 (top): © Linnell Esler, www.sxc.hu, reprinted with permission

(background): Edmar Júnior, www.sxc.hu, reprinted with permission

124: © JR Goleno, www.sxc.hu, reprinted with permission

126: © Dave Sackville, www.sxc.hu, reprinted with permission

127: © medinamaga, www.sxc.hu, reprinted with permission

128 (Oliver Schroer): © Michael Wrycraft

128–29 (background): © Joel Terrell, www.sxc.hu, reprinted with permission

131: © janet goulden, www.sxc.hu, reprinted with permission

132: © Jean Scheijen, www.sxc.hu, reprinted with permission

134 (Hal Niedzviecki): © Sam Niedzviecki

135: © istockphoto.com/Edward Hor

136–37: album art by Annie Wilkinson, band photo by Dawna Humble/Sears Portrait Studio. Courtesy of Duplex

139 (top): © Merrit Rawsthorne

(bottom): © Paul Preacher, www.sxc.hu, reprinted with permission

140–41: © Jean Scheijen, www.sxc.hu, reprinted with permission

142 (top): © Tyson Fast

(bottom) © istockphoto.com/Simon Podgorsek

(background) Rodolfo Clix, www.sxc.hu, reprinted with permission

143: Courtesy of You Say Party We Say Die

144: © istockphoto.com/Jelani Memory

146 (photo of hands): © istockphoto.com

148: © Georgios M. W., www.sxc.hu, reprinted with permission

150: Youthful radio expert, 1922. Prints and Photographs Division, Library of Congress, LC-USZ62-93539

151: Dairy farmer tuning radio, 1923. Prints and Photographs Division, Library of Congress, LC-USZ62-60682

152: © istockphoto.com/Curt Pickens

(background): blue sky, www.sxc.hu, reprinted with permission

155: Wireless kit in Brooklyn radio shop, 1922. Prints and Photographs Division, Library of Congress, LC-USZ62-78078

156: © Dangerous Boy, www.sxc.hu, reprinted with permission

157: © Keith Syvinski, www.sxc.hu, reprinted with permission

158: © Jonathan Edwards, www.sxc.hu, reprinted with permission

159: © Nicole Shackelford, www.sxc.hu, reprinted with permission

161: © Christopher Grondahl, www.sxc.hu, reprinted with permission

162 (top left): © istockphoto.com/Chris Schmidt

(background) Wireless station, 1916. Frank and Frances Carpenter Collection, Prints and Photographs Division, Library of Congress (no reproduction number)

165: © Pedro Alvarado, www.sxc.hu, reprinted with permission

166–67 (buttons): Courtesy of *Broken Pencil* magazine

168 (bottom): © Marco Michelini, www.sxc.hu, reprinted with permission

169: Courtesy Sherwin Tija

170: © Steve Carboni, www.sxc.hu, reprinted with permission

171: Courtesy Joe Biel

172–73: Courtesy secretfunspot.com, images supplied by Kirk Demarais

174: © istockphoto.com/Arpad Benedek

175: © istockphoto.com/Arthur Kwiatkowski

(bottom): © Konrado Fedorczyko, www.sxc.hu, reprinted with permission

INDEX

accessibility, 15–17
amateur radio, 151, 155

Backyard Wrestling Federation
    (BYWF), 162
The Barmitzvah Brothers, 131
Beehive, Betty, 17
Biel, Joe, 171
Bleek, 154
blog, blogging, 43, 169
book production, 92, 95–96
Bourret, Iza, 93
Broken Pencil, 7, 8, 9

cable community access
    channels, 163–64
celebrity worship, Celebrity
    Worship Syndrome, 66
censor, censorship, 30, 32
Chapman, Jeff, 90
chat rooms, 169
Cinderella, 27–28
cool, 44
copyright, 108–9, 144, 159
Cornflake Rebellion, 82
corporate pop culture, 22, 37–44,
    46–50, 55, 57, 59–62
culture, 14
culture jamming, 61, 65, 107

distribution networks (Internet, TV,
    radio), independent distribution,
    148–61, 175–76
distros, 170–72
DIY pop culture, 54–73, 126
    history of, 54–59
    manifesto, 72
documentary, 103, 106, 114
Dracula, 20
Duplex, 136–37
Duppy, 87

Earnhart, Stephen, 103
ediaries, 169, 174

Fanning, Shawn, 144
file sharing, file trading, 144
film, 106
focus groups, 50
folk culture, 24–30, 32, 43

Ford, Victoria, 103
Found, 83

genre, 22, 104–5
Goldirocks, 120–21
"gonzo" journalism, 55
Gutenberg, Johannes, 21

ham radio, 157
The Happy Loner, 93
Hard Rock Academy, 141
high culture, 20

independent/indie pop culture,
    37–39, 42–43, 46–50, 59–60, 65
independent/indie television
    broadcasting, 162–68
Industrial Revolution, 25
Infiltration, 90
Internet radio, 143, 155–57

Kiss Machine, 70–71

listservs, 169–79
Lucasfilm, 109

mass production, 15–17, 55
McLaren, Carrie, 48
Menon, Vinay, 45
Merritt Free Cast Radio (MFCR), 154
Microcosm Publishing, 171
motion pictures, 102–23
    screening, 119, 122
moving picture photography,
    105, 107
Mule Skinner Blues, 103

Napster, 144

Oswald, John, 65
The Overspent American, 40

personal computer, 58–59
"Phantom Edit," 109
pirate radio, 143, 149–55, 157, 162
playing live music, 138–42
plunder, 65, 107, 129, 167
Plunderphonics, 65
podcast, 143, 157–59, 162

Pohl-Weary, Emily, 70–71
pop culture, 7–9, 14–33
    cheat sheet, 17
    history of, 21–30
    hysteria and moral panic,
        29–31
    timeline, 23
pop music, 126–45
    getting heard, 142–44
    playing live, 138–42
    recording, 132–38
pop song, 128
Popular Culture: A User's Guide, 18
printing press, 21
product placement, 40, 44
Purins, Ansis, 87

recording, 132–38
Rich, Friendly, 56
Rothbart, Davy, 83

sampled song, 129
Schor, Juliet, 40
script writing, 108, 110
scripted story, 106
self-publishing, 78, 87, 94–95, 171
songwriting, 129–32
sound song, 129
Stay Free, 48
Szeman, Imre, 18–19

Tiberius, Paula, 120–21

underground culture, 55

Verri, Kris, 165
video, 106
video games, 172–73

War of the Worlds, 30, 31
websites, 168–75
webzines, 169
writing, 69, 78–81, 85, 108, 110, 120

zine, 78–79, 81–93
    distribution, 96–98

About the Author

Hal Niedzviecki is a pop culture fan who cherishes his childhood collection of *Incredible Hulk* comics and *Star Wars* action figures. (He once put Han Solo in the microwave and turned it on, but that's another story.) He grew up in Ottawa, Ontario, and in the suburbs of Washington, D.C. Now he lives in Toronto, Ontario, where he plays music, runs a magazine, and writes articles and books. A culture critic and fiction writer, he's either reading zines and comics, watching or playing hockey, or looking for that lost important scrap of paper (he's really got to clean up his office). To find out more about Hal's work, visit his website www.smellit.ca or send him an email at hal@brokenpencil.com.

About Broken Pencil: The Magazine of Zine Culture and the Independent Arts

Broken Pencil is a mega-zine founded in 1995 by Hal Niedzviecki and Hilary Clark. Now published four times a year, each issue of the (mega)zine features reviews of zines, independent film and video, small press books, comics, websites, artworks, music, and more. The magazine also reprints from the best of the independent press and runs articles on everything from pirate radio to grrrl culture. To find out more about BP, go to www.brokenpencil.com.